Make Your Business Social

Make Your Business Social

Engage Your Customers with Social Media

Lindsay Chambers, Jennifer Morehead, and Heather Sallee

BEP BUSINESS EXPERT PRESS

First published in 2020 by
Business Expert Press, LLC
222 East 46th Street, New York, NY 10017
www.businessexpertpress.com

ISBN-13: 978-1-95253-800-1 (paperback)
ISBN-13: 978-1-95253-801-8 (e-book)

Business Expert Press Digital and Social Media Marketing and Advertising Collection

Collection ISSN: 2333-8822 (print)
Collection ISSN: 2333-8830 (electronic)

Cover image licensed by Ingram Image, StockPhotoSecrets.com
Cover and interior design by S4Carlisle Publishing Services Private Ltd., Chennai, India

First edition: 2020

10 9 8 7 6 5 4 3 2 1

Printed in the United States of America.

We dedicate this book to the Salesboxer customers who trust us to help them grow. We profoundly appreciate the opportunity to work closely with you each day. Also, we are grateful to the business owners who contributed their thoughts and experience to our featured case studies. Finally, we have a few personal dedications to make.

Lindsay Chambers: To my husband Paul, my partner and best friend, thank you for your unwavering love and support.

Jennifer Morehead: To my loving and always fun "fraternity" family, including my husband Brad and three boys.

Heather Sallee: To my husband, who tolerates my wild ideas, DIY home projects, and marketing talk.

Abstract

Social media has exploded, not only for individuals but for businesses too. Today, more than 83% of small business owners say they believe social media is essential for their companies. *Make Your Business Social* provides actionable solutions for business owners to create and sustain a successful social media presence.

In *Make Your Business Social* you will learn how to

- Build or expand a social media audience for your business.
- Create graphics, even if you're not a designer.
- Choose the right platforms for your business.
- Cultivate strategies for present and future social media.
- Use real-life experience from current business owners.

Make Your Business Social brings fresh insights from its three authors, who have spent years creating and managing social media for businesses. Within these pages, you will find the inspiration you need to expand your social media presence and add an appealing new dimension to your branding and marketing efforts.

Keywords

social media marketing; business marketing; social media; e-mail marketing; salesboxer; marketing; digital marketing; digital marketing plan; business advertising; advertising; branding; content marketing; Facebook; Twitter; Instagram; LinkedIn; YouTube; social media advertising; manage social media; manage social media for business; marketing plan; setting up social media for marketing; best social media platforms for businesses; free marketing for small businesses; social media for small business owners

Contents

Introduction

By now, almost everyone on the planet has experienced some form of social media. Social media, of course, is a somewhat newer mode of communication than the invention of hieroglyphics, Morse code, or the telephone but won't be going away anytime soon. Social media, whether you personally like it or not, has become necessary for every business communicating with their audience.

The evidence speaks for itself: When you figure out how to share the human aspect of your business and the lives you have touched through it, people buy into not only what you are selling, but also into your story as a business. It turns out that having an audience that buys into your story is always good for business.

Today, more than 83 percent of small business owners say they believe social media is essential for their business. We have put this book together to ensure you have the best plan and approach to win at social media.

We can all agree social media is polarizing. Fake news, changing platforms, and password management can all be frustrating. Social media harnesses the excitement of extroverts, who like to have continuous conversations. It highlights the reluctance of introverts, who might feel like it's an invasion during private moments. Social media also gives a platform to the jerks of the world, who use it to troll others and show us the fun we aren't having and the vacations we are missing.

On the other hand, social media is a tremendous way to connect. During the COVID-19 outbreak, businesses found that social media was a crucial way to stay in touch with their customers. Social media allows for old high school friends to connect updated about one another's lives. You can view pictures of your nieces' and nephews' birthday parties, even if you can't be there for those moments. Social media can open the doors to make meaningful connections with others during a pandemic or in normal circumstances.

If you don't care for social media, don't worry. This book is not going to talk you into liking social media for yourself. Our book will not address whether social media should or should not exist. We have put this introduction together to explain that we understand the feelings around social media, both good and bad, but you will have to save those comments for watercooler conversations at work, the Thanksgiving dinner table, and online comment sections.

You may wonder: "Why another book on using social media for business?" If you check the bookshelves of your local bookstore, you will see a sleek selection of books offering quick tips or a single strategy for marketing your business through social media. Our book offers a different approach. Our tips aren't just theoretical; they are tested and true.

We want to take you behind the scenes and share with you our success stories working with many different businesses, along with the stories of others. We have connected with numerous small business owners just like you, who have grown steadily over the years by having an intentional social media presence.

Who should be interested in this book? In short, everyone. But especially those who run a business or online brand. We fight for the little guy. We understand what it's like to start out or feel stuck—for instance, no matter what you do, your business is surviving at best. We also know the road to getting unstuck, as we have traveled it with many clients.

For example, let's say you are a plumber in your community. You've distinguished yourself from your competition by steadily building a reputation for high-quality work at fair prices. You don't quite grasp how to use social media to build your business, but you know you need a steady, growing stream of customers. Many of your potential clients spend a considerable amount of time on social media, but you don't know how to connect to them and continue the conversation to build awareness around your brand.

Or perhaps you install pavers and hardscapes to upgrade home patios and lay asphalt and cement to help brick-and-mortar businesses get more customers. You have a ton of before-and-after pictures of job sites you'd love to showcase on social media, but you have no idea where to start.

What if you run a doctor's office? You have interesting content to share and ways to position yourself as a leading expert in your field. However, you don't have the time, and your office doesn't have the experience, to strategically maintain your social platforms.

Maybe you own a moving company. Most people don't get passionate about moving in the same way they enjoy cooking, decorating, or working out. Often, people find the topic of moving stressful and would prefer not to think about it. But you run a business that relies on a steady customer base, and the traditional ways of finding those customers aren't working.

What if you are a spirited college-aged woman with an amazing YouTube following because you do makeup application tutorials? People love to follow you because you are funny and self-deprecating and they learn how to make themselves look better. However, you want a better strategy to monetize this following.

Our book pulls together stories from companies that have had a lot of success, along with our take on how to harness the best of what social media has to offer. We have put together easy-to-digest concepts to help you visualize where you and your company belong on the social media landscape.

Look at the following chart for a visual representation of the different platforms. We will explore this further in the book, but think of your business and where it might fit on this chart. Are you a design business that is more visual and focused on entertainment? Or perhaps you are a consulting company that could benefit from more text and news. We will help break down the concepts of social media to make them easy and actionable for you (Figure 0.1).

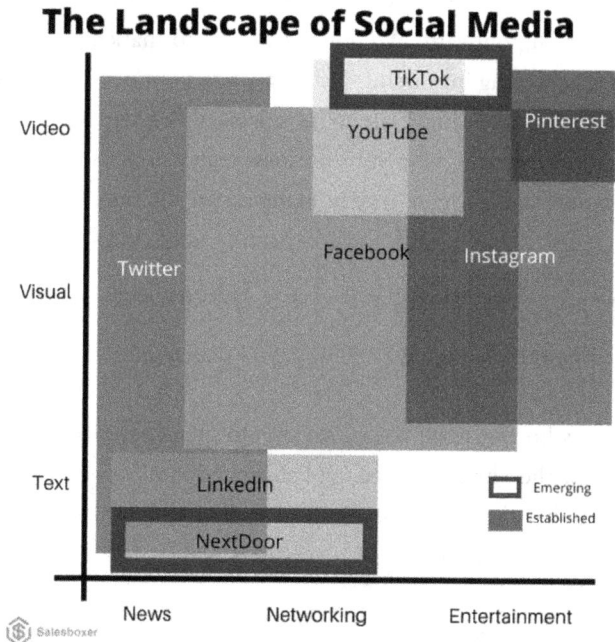

Figure 0.1 The landscape of social media

At the end of our book, in Chapter 10, we will talk about emerging platforms and trends. Some of those emerging platforms, especially as they pertain to businesses, include TikTok and NextDoor (both pictured in the landscape) in addition to Snapchat, Quora, and Reddit. While these platforms aren't brand-new, they are emerging in terms of how we perceive businesses are approaching them to build their brands. We work primarily with businesses that target people 25 years old and older. Businesses that hope to attract a younger demographic must pay even closer attention to the emerging platforms. The platforms we focus on in this book include Facebook, Instagram, Pinterest, Twitter, LinkedIn, and YouTube. Many of the lessons and ideas we teach for these platforms are also applicable to the newer, smaller, or emerging ones as well.

We want to share our story with you and help you discover yours. Remember the enthusiasm and drive that helped you start your business? We want you to channel that and share it with the world through social media. The evidence speaks for itself: When you figure out how to share the human aspect of your business and the lives you have touched through it, people buy into not only what you are selling, but also your company's story.

Our process is more organic than most, starting with your core values and working outward. We don't want you to market yourself in an artificial way, buying into trends just to get a rise out of people. We want you to dare to be genuine. Dare to be a classic. We are going to go on an exciting trip of sharing who your business truly is on social media, and your customers are going to love it. Hang on for the ride.

Introduction: Key Takeaways

After reading this chapter, what should you understand?

1. Those who run small businesses should spend time on social media to grow their brands, reach, and customer base.
2. Remember the landscape of social media, and don't try to take on too much too soon.

3. You can start with just one or two platforms, but be strategic about which one(s) you choose.
4. Social media is valuable for businesses because it humanizes their brand and allows their personality to shine.
5. This book will provide real-world examples of businesses that have done a good job of establishing a presence on one or more platforms.

CHAPTER 1

Why Spend the Time on Social Media?

Social media is about entering into a conversation with a diverse group of people who could buy your product or service, refer you to a friend, or enjoy the content you put out there and be your customer in 5 years. Each business, whether it's made up of one person or 1,000 people, has something special and immensely personal at the heart of it. You can take your business to the next level by unlocking the magic of social media and its power to connect your ideas, culture, and mission to a broader community (Figure 1.1).

Figure 1.1 Social media is all around us

In Chapter 2, we're going to start getting interactive with you and asking questions about the particular social media needs of your business. But here, in Chapter 1, we'll get right to the point to convince you of the need for social media. Social media acts as a focus group for your business, an easier and cheaper form of advertising, creates customer loyalty in ways you wouldn't believe, and helps you build your brand. Now you understand why it's become so popular and necessary for businesses.

We will do our best to explain all of what social media can do for your business, but first, we're going to give you the key takeaways of the entire book for those of you in a hurry. After all, you can't be an expert in everything, because you are busy being an expert in running your business. Here are our key takeaways for social media that we'll detail in the pages to come.

Key Takeaways throughout the Book

1. Remember the landscape of social media, and be strategic about which ones you choose to use for your business. Don't spread yourself too thin.
2. Use fun and noncontroversial topics in the broader pop culture realm to look for questions to ask your audience, to get them into the practice of answering on your social media platform.
3. You can use the responses to your posts to determine, in real time, what resonates with your audience and what does not.
4. Use hashtags creatively to build your brand and set your business apart from the competition.
5. Get personal with the story behind your business. Your audience will appreciate the authenticity.
6. If you're just getting started with social media, focus on one platform at a time to avoid taking on too much at once.
7. Cultivate an audience by starting with current customers.
8. Develop a strategy and be intentional with what you post.
9. Use graphics to grab users' attention, maximize the impact of what you post, and help you stand out in the crowded landscape of social media.
10. You don't need a degree in design to create clean, professional-looking graphics. Plenty of websites offer free software to help with this.

11. Don't make every post a sales pitch. Mix it up with content that shows a more personable side of your business. Use graphics wherever possible.

12. It may take some trial and error to find the ideal times of day and frequency to post content.

13. You can create Facebook ads to get highly targeted with your audience. Facebook advertising doesn't have to be expensive. You can reach hundreds of people for a few dollars a day.

14. Use the power of LinkedIn groups to generate new leads. Join groups that are relevant to your business, and become part of the conversation. Post articles that demonstrate your expertise.

15. YouTube is free to use and has virtually no barriers to entry, making it an ideal platform for small businesses trying to grow their online brand on a shoestring budget.

16. People find video content engaging and memorable and will spend time watching videos you post, though shorter clips (1 minute or less) are usually more effective.

17. Be sure to include keywords and calls to action in every video you upload.

18. You can gain a following on Twitter by using hashtags creatively, following and engaging with influencers, and posting several times a day.

19. Use Twitter lists to keep up with competitors, boost your relationships with industry leaders, and stay abreast of trends and news.

20. It's smart to stay on top of emerging social platforms, in addition to maintaining an active presence on established ones such as Facebook and LinkedIn.

21. Find microinfluencers within your niche or industry, and reach out to explore a partnership.

22. Use your logo when posting visual content.

23. Many different companies have found success in sharing funny, relatable posts featuring photos of their staff or customers interacting with their products.

These are the high points of our book. As you know, though, the devil is in the details, and we'd like to explain more. Let's jump back into how social media can benefit your business through a built-in focus group, advertising, customer loyalty program, and brand building all in one.

Focus Group Created Just for Your Business

Have you ever launched a product or service you thought would be wildly popular but wasn't? Think about the time, energy, and expense you put into creating it, and how much you might have benefited from bouncing the idea off the right customers who could have pointed you in the right direction. Social media is a focus group that is tailored just for you and your company. As long as you nurture and reward your audience and followers, you will get their honest, and instant, feedback. Fantastic.

People love to give their opinions on things, especially when they feel like they aren't obligated to give them. You can start by asking people on your social media page to weigh in on how they feel about an upcoming football game or popular TV show, among your other posts. Use fun and noncontroversial topics in the broader pop culture realm to look for questions. Then, get into the habit of offering a small reward for audience members who are willing to share their thoughts. Take it to the next level by asking a more controversial question and watching the comments spike—you need to do this carefully, though.

One example of an easy, inoffensive example of a question most people have strong opinions on is which way to hang the toilet paper roll: over or under. You get the idea. You can start to sprinkle in questions about your business, and, presto, you have some quick and easy answers, directly from your customers.

Advertising Made Easy(er)

Can you recall an advertising campaign you launched long ago in the Yellow Pages (remember those?), or, more recently, on Google Adwords? Many business owners waste a ton of money on ineffective advertising until they finally hit on a strategy that works. Advertising can be more art than science, and it's tricky to get it right. As your audience grows, posting your advertisements, features, and specials on social media can become a cheaper and easier option than advertising. You can advertise seasonal offers or something that is more regular. You can see in real time what flops and what resonates with your audience.

Big-Time Customer Loyalty

Remember loyalty card programs? They were a strategy companies used to stay top of mind every time their customers opened their wallets, as well as to collect information from people at checkout.

Your audience on social media can essentially function as a vast, ongoing customer loyalty program. When your customers are looking at their favorite social media platforms, they will be able to see your posts, have insider access to specials you post, and feel as if they are part of what you're doing. Social media is a built-in customer loyalty program for your business. You can track who your super users are through your pages and understand the preferences of your customer without the cost of the loyalty program and all the badgering by sales representatives.

Build Your Brand

As a smaller business, it can feel like a nearly insurmountable challenge to break through the chatter and clatter of your competitors. Regardless of the industry, or subset of the industry, there are always multiple options for customers to pick. How do you set yourself apart?

Social media provides an inexpensive way to experiment and develop your brand within your corner of the Internet. Use logos and visual graphics to attract your customers. We feel it's also essential to create a few company-specific hashtags and use them consistently in your posts. Hashtags help further define what you're discussing and create a consistent branding technique. Get creative with the pound sign and your words. Some examples that we use include #salesboxersells and #salesboxersocial.

For hashtags, we put together a strategy for each of our clients. Our hashtag strategy includes creating customized hashtags around the company's brand, customized hashtags for their products, and popular trending hashtags that could help the company show up in a broader search. We log on to Instagram and try different hashtags to see how many searches they produce, then use that information to determine the best hashtags to use.

Remember, content is cheap and there is a lot of it out there. If you're going to go to the work of populating one or more social media platforms, you need to make sure your brand is immediately noticeable at first glance.

Chapter 1: Key Takeaways

After reading this chapter, what should you understand?

1. Social media provides an opportunity to create stronger customer loyalty by connecting your brand with the world.
2. You can use the responses to your posts to determine, in real time, what resonates with your audience and what does not.
3. Use fun and noncontroversial topics in the broader pop culture realm to look for questions to ask your audience, to get them into the practice of answering on your social media platform.
4. Put hashtags together based on the company, products, and overall searches for particular terms.
5. Be patient with social media. It might take several tries to hit on something that sticks, and that's OK.

CHAPTER 2

Take It Offline to Develop Your Social Media Content

The most daunting part of getting started in social media is thinking about the personality and actual content of your posts. Facebook asks us, "What's on your mind?" to prompt the content for a post. For some, that comes naturally, but others can get massive writer's block. In this chapter, we will identify easy ways to come up with content for your social media posts. At the end, we'll provide examples of how to put together a broader marketing strategy, but we need to start with easy sources for your social media content. We will distill the very essence of what makes you, your brand, and your company tick.

Define What Makes You Special

When we start working with clients to develop their social media audience from scratch, we often start by asking them some questions. Go ahead and answer the questions below. Trust us, it will only take a minute.

- Why do customers work with you?
- What makes you get up on Monday morning looking forward to what you're doing?
- When and why did you start your business?
- What is your favorite part of what you do?
- What is your clients' favorite thing to order from you?
- What inspires you to keep going?

As you answer these questions, you should start to see some golden nuggets show through. Why is your dental practice the one people will choose for their whole family? What about your consulting practice helps you stand apart from the rest? What makes your hair salon the best for women who want to maintain their cut and color?

Once you have identified the heart of what makes your company special, you can work on accentuating and refining it. Start by identifying the feel and flavor of your company and brand. Take a moment to answer these questions.

- Is your brand/company lighthearted and fun, silly and irreverent, or more serious and informative?
- Do your products or services naturally lend themselves to compelling photography, or are you seeking pictures outside of what you do to create a story? Think of a cosmetics business versus a moving company.
- What do your customers love most about what you do?
- Where do your company and brand draw inspiration?

Think through these answers to the question of what makes your company special, and use them to fuel the basis of what you'll write on social media. Feel free to brag about yourself a little. Tell others all the complimentary things other people have said about you.

Expose Your Company's Watercooler

Now that you've identified what makes your company special, let's add to it by thinking of your company's watercooler. Let's split this into businesses with employees in one place versus businesses that employ remote teams or are solopreneurships (like freelance writers or photographers). During and after the COVID-19 pandemic, many businesses have had to adjust to their teams working remotely, so pay particular attention to the second part of this section.

If you have employees, answer a few of these questions.

- Where do they most often gather to talk about what's going on?
- What do they talk about?
- Which employees are the most influential to the overall team?

An easy way to find inspiration about what to discuss on social media is to expose this company watercooler talk. If there's a debate in the office about something mundane that might not have anything to do with your mission, it could be interesting to post as a question or poll on social media. Remember, your posts don't always need to be about what you do. Since your goal is to build relationships, it's better to maintain friendly conversations with your audience instead of always trying to ram your latest offer down their throats.

But what if your company is just you or if your team consists of people working remotely? It is entirely possible to build team culture from afar. You can have Zoom townhall meetings or Zoom trivia events where people can just hang out online and personalities can shine through. Give everyone who works with you access to your content calendar and the login credentials to schedule posts. You can double-check to make sure the posts are appropriate before they go live. You can also stay on top of current events and create a "watercooler" environment for your brand, even if you work alone.

Tell Your Company's Story

We have identified what makes your company special and hot topics that happen around your company's watercooler, and now we're going to focus that into your company's story. What was a story you heard recently that stuck with you? Chances are, it connected with you in some way. Whether it tugged at your heartstrings to feel compassion for someone, made you angry on behalf of another, or inspired you to try something new, it was meaningful because it felt relevant to your experience. That is the type of story you want to share with your clientele.

When telling your story, you don't want to preach. A good story has an implied message or theme. It has a beginning, a middle, and an end. There is a problem (or several) to solve in a climactic moment or two. Ideally, it has a happy ending. Your business should be the solution to the problem, but you don't want to jump in with that first.

Instead, start at the beginning: One day, your average working mother finishes work and finds ants crawling all over her kitchen counter. They gobble greedily on the graham cracker crumbs her son left there. She thoroughly cleans the counter and the sink. Two days later, the ants return. They found their way back to the spot they had found before, even though there was no food there. What will the mother do?

In her hour of need, she picks up the phone and dials the number of your exterminator business. Her heart races with delight the next day, as you show up on time and deliver exceptional service. You have saved the day. She is smiling as your van pulls out of her driveway, because she knows her home matters to you. You put in the extra effort and were conscientious about spraying and setting the appropriate traps throughout the house. You were personable, polite, and reassuring.

When that is the kind of story you can tell about your business, customers will be drawn to you like those ants to the graham crackers. Your values will naturally shine through in the narrative you tell.

Maybe you don't have a wealth of customer experience to share yet, but everyone has an inspiring story. Instead, you could tell people why you were so excited to start this company in the first place.

Ever since you were 10 years old and you picked up your first saxophone, you were hooked. You discovered the magic of music, and your world wasn't the same ever since. You joined the school band and performed in every concert. You were making new friends and gaining self-confidence.

Then, the unthinkable happened. Your dog chewed the mouthpiece so badly that you couldn't play saxophone with it anymore. With no place within reasonable distance to get it repaired, and not enough money to do so, you gave up playing the saxophone for over a year until you could buy a new one.

As an adult, you now offer a unique, in-home instrument repair service. You've learned how to do everything from tuning a piano to stringing a guitar. You have a unique set of skills and a passion to enable others to continue in their musical endeavors. Let your journey inspire others.

So, what is your story? What did you tell your uncle last Christmas when he asked you what you do for a living for the umpteenth time? How can you share the story of your business with others? It's time to start practicing. Sharing your story will be an essential, ongoing process in having an impactful social media presence.

Develop Content from What We All Have in Common

When you start putting content online about your business, you will also find the best-performing posts aren't always about your company. Many of the most engaging posts are about fun topics that exist in the general

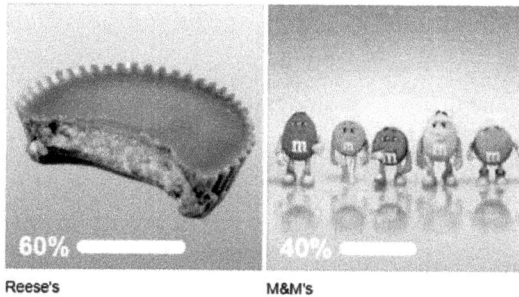

Figure 2.1 Which is your favorite?

realm of pop culture or common, noncontroversial holidays. Find shared, broad experiences, and make these posts engaging! Not all your posts should be about heavy, sophisticated topics. See the following example about favorite Halloween candy (Figure 2.1).

Examples of questions you could ask around noncontroversial holidays:

- What is your favorite Thanksgiving dish?
- What do you like to do on Labor Day?
- Who stays up until midnight on New Year's Eve?

Examples of questions you could ask about events in popular culture:

- What team will win the Super Bowl?
- What is your favorite song of the summer?

- What is your favorite memory from when you were a kid?

Now, we have a robust base for drawing content for your social media platforms. We have talked about what makes your company special, telling your company's story, and drawing from things we all have in common. Use the answers to your questions, and you have a "plug-and-play" start for content on social media.

Create a Marketing Plan for Your Business

A marketing strategy is essential for all businesses because it serves as a step-by-step road map to promote your products and services and get more sales. You will need to outline specific goals for your business, do research about how to accomplish the goals, and then identify the tactics, money, and time that will go toward accomplishing the goals. We will do a quick overview of a broader marketing plan but then narrow our focus to show how it should specifically apply to social media.

For the most successful approach to goal-setting for your marketing strategy, remember the acronym SMART:

- Specific
- Measurable
- Achievable
- Realistic
- Time-bound

In other words, it's not enough to set a vague goal like "Our business will attract and retain new customers." Instead, define objectives such as "We will grow our customer base by 25 percent by the end of the first quarter of the fiscal year." This level of specificity will help you keep track of your progress and determine any opportunities for improvement.

Ask yourself the following questions to develop a marketing strategy:

- If your business goal is to grow revenue, what marketing objectives will accomplish this?

- What is the most efficient way to attract more customers, by gaining word-of-mouth credibility or finding better lead sources?
- What money and time do you or your employees have to spend on growing revenue?

Market research and analysis are crucial in developing a successful marketing plan, but many businesses overlook this step. Conducting research doesn't have to be complicated or unattainably expensive. The Internet has leveled the playing field by putting many resources within easy reach. You can also organize customer focus groups as an inexpensive way to get to know your target audience and what challenges your product or service can help them solve.

Next, create a detailed overview of your marketing strategies, and list each of the corresponding tactics you'll employ to execute them. To return to the previous example of growing your customer base by 25 percent by the end of the first quarter of the fiscal year, one of your tactics might be to create a targeted e-mail list of your prospects, and market to them with a monthly newsletter. Maybe, in addition to the e-mail strategy, you identify Google Adwords and social media as a three-pronged effort to attract customers and grow sales.

The tactics section of your marketing plan should outline all the actionable steps you plan to take for advertising and promoting your business. Write these steps down, and be sure to follow through on each one.

In the final section of your marketing plan, outline the money and time you will budget for each of your tactics. So, if you're going to create an online marketing campaign, include the costs associated with designing and placing the ads, as well as the amount you will pay to run the ads on your chosen platform. If you project that the tactics you've selected will exceed your budget, this is the step where you'll revise them.

Our book is, of course, focused on social media, so we will take a moment to drill down on the tactic within your marketing strategy of expanding your social media reach. In addition to the content that you have identified to post, you will want to identify how often you will post, and what platforms you will use to reach your customers. In Chapter 11, you will read case studies that show how other business owners like you have approached the strategy of their social media efforts.

Your marketing plan is never set in stone. Indeed, it's a living, breathing document that can grow and change alongside you as your business evolves. Soon, you'll find it's a tool you can't afford to be without.

Chapter 2: Key Takeaways

After reading this chapter, what should you understand?

1. Social media is a focus group tailored to your business. It enables real-time analysis of what your audience likes and doesn't like.
2. Use hashtags creatively to build your brand and set your business apart from the competition.
3. Decide what content to share and how often to post by asking yourself a few pivotal questions.
4. Get personal with the story behind your business. Your audience will appreciate the authenticity.
5. Take time to develop a marketing plan that will grow with your business.

CHAPTER 3

Cultivate an Audience

It may be easy to set up social media pages, but it is another thing altogether to build your audience. Some of us are blessed with witty online banter abilities, but most of us, sadly, are not. You will need to rely on some on-the-ground tactics to build your audience and make sure they remain engaged. Even if you can regularly whip out fun and engaging posts by relying on our tactics, you will most likely need some patience as your online audience grows.

You'll need to find the right people to engage if you are going to spend the time and money to do so. Be thoughtful about the sphere of influencers for your company. Consider these elements:

- What geographic area is the best one for you to target?
- Are your customers male, female, or both?
- And what are their ages?
- What are the passions and interests of people who buy what your business sells?
- Who refers you to your best clients?

These are straightforward questions about your audience, but depending on what you do, you can work to get more and more specific. Think about the composite of your ideal customer, then tailor the content that you've envisioned to that individual.

Choose a Foundation Platform, Then Add Others

We recommend that you focus on only one social media platform as your foundation and then grow your audience with additional platforms. Which one is your favorite? If you aren't already a regular user of social media for your business, we suggest Facebook as a starting point. It's the most developed social media platform, it has the largest audience, and it is easy for customers to reach you. But you are the business owner, so if you already enjoy a social media platform, that is also a good bet for the one that should become your foundation.

Next, you can think about one or more avenues you'd like to develop beyond your first foundational platform. Think about what's right for your brand. For example, if you run an Etsy store where you sell customized party décor and favors, you could combine Facebook with Instagram, since these are both highly visual platforms.

When we start working with clients, we identify the best platforms for them. We pull compelling photos that will work in their promotions and content. We determine what kinds of fresh content to promote to keep audiences interested and engaged. We also think about other partners we can cross-promote, who may in turn cross-promote for our clients' pages. Finally, we put together a document that has all the URLs for the pages we've created, the login credentials for those pages, and a way to track the social media platform growth.

The landscape of social media is always changing, so we won't ever be able to capture an exhaustive overview of each platform, but here is an overview of what we believe to be the most relevant social media platforms for your business.

- *Facebook*: Encompasses video, visual, and text and spans news, networking, and entertainment. It's an established platform, and customers can easily reach out to you and interact with your brand.
- *Twitter*: Focused on the news and encompasses video, visual, and text. You can find trending hashtags on Twitter and often retweet a post or tag someone in a post to interact with them.
- *Instagram*: A visual medium that incorporates pictures, graphics, and videos that are mainly focused on entertainment. Young women and moms are still very excited about Instagram.
- *YouTube*: Focused on networking and entertainment through video. You can easily make a short video, usually around 1 minute or less, and post within a channel on YouTube that is dedicated to your brand.

- *LinkedIn*: Focused on news and networking and is mainly filled with text-heavy posts with some graphics and pictures. You can find business-to-business leads here, potential partnerships, or recruiting help for your business.
- *Pinterest*: General interest and focused on pictures and graphics in the entertainment sphere. People use it to identify favorite outfits, decorating tips, and the like. We have found it's harder for the average small business to use this platform for marketing, unless they are highly visual.
- *NextDoor*: An emerging social media platform that is text-heavy and focused on news and networking within specific neighborhoods.
- *TikTok*: An emerging social media platform that is primarily video used for networking and entertainment.

Nurture Your Fan Base

Whether you've been in business for 20 years or only getting started, it's essential for you to have an audience and to continue to speak to them consistently. As you set out on your social media strategy, it's helpful to cultivate your audience by building on any existing fan base.

Who is your audience? Maybe it's your average, middle-class homeowner, looking for a repair tech. Or perhaps, as a local tutor, you cater to parents who want to make sure their children are getting a quality education. Do you own a day spa? Target people who have a stressful lifestyle and could use a massage.

Make sure you identify your target audience to understand their world, and why they need what you have to offer. Here's where you get to show them how you shine.

If you have been in business for some time, use your current customers to build your social media audience. Send your past and current customers an e-mail with an incentive to like your Facebook page and other social platforms. You can link to your social media pages from your website to make it easy for existing and potential customers to join you online.

If you are new to your business, use any audience of people who like you and believe in what you do. Maybe it's a personal Instagram following, or your aunts and uncles who are on Facebook. Share your new business social media accounts with everyone.

Incentivize and Make It Fun

Social media can be an enjoyable place to spend time, especially if you are promoting a business. Your business might characteristically have a fun, irreverent brand, tone, and audience, which makes it easier to post and build your audience. Or you might have a more buttoned-up nature, such as a medical billing company trying to show credibility to doctor's offices. However, regardless of your brand and its identity, you will enjoy building your audience by staying true to the roots of your company.

Building your audience becomes less daunting when you realize that social media is not constrictive or permanent. You can immediately delete or edit anything you put out in the social media ether. Next, social media is incredibly visual. Even businesses with limited financial or technical resources can use something as simple as PowerPoint to put together a reasonably professional-looking graphic, using your logo and a picture from a free stock photo site like Pexels, and voilà, you have something impactful.

People are on social media to have fun and invest their time in passions and hobbies that interest them. They are also there to network with friends, family, or colleagues. No matter what you do, you can create enjoyable incentives for your audience to connect with their interests through your company. For example, we have a client that puts together special movie premiere nights for their staff and social media followers. Have fun with the incentives you develop to get people engaging with your pages and your content.

On the flip side of the fun incentive technique for social media, comes the ability to show the heart of your business. During the COVID-19 pandemic, restaurants created promotions where they served free food to doctors, nurses, and essential workers. Various businesses also ran campaigns during the pandemic where they would offer video content in exchange for a donation to a food bank.

Monitor and Measure Success

We hear from a lot of clients who ask us how they should measure their success on social media. There's no one correct answer to that question. The various industries, and individual companies within each, make it a challenge to generalize success in social media. There are also different ways business owners define success of social media. Some companies might have a sales process that closely tracks how a lead came in, but in most cases, they don't. Some business owners might feel that success looks like landing a significant client using social media, while others are just thrilled to have the added credibility of pages they can promote on their website.

We recommend some tools that make it easier to help put metrics around your social media efforts.

One of these is Urchin Tracking Module, or UTM. These are codes that help you track your marketing with Google Analytics. They enable you to follow various kinds of information such as how people found your ads and what types of searches allowed them to find you. You can try out different keywords and types of ads to see which ones perform better. Google allows you to build URLs that you can tweak along the way to track all your ad campaigns.[1]

Often, you can find analytics feedback to tell you how successful your posts are and to track trends through a section called "Insights." On Facebook, for example, if you click on the "Insights" tab of your business page, you can get easy updates on various levels of engagement your page has had, including its reach, views, and engagement. If you scroll down, you can see how each post performed in these same categories.

Within Facebook Insights, you can choose whether you want to give specific posts a boost. At the bottom, there is a section called "Pages to Watch," which shows you similar Facebook pages and compares their performance with yours. This feature can help you see what you need to do to compete, or can give you ideas for some types of posts you want to try.

Similarly, on Instagram, you can view insights on your business account. These will give you information about specific posts or help you learn more about your followers. You can view by week how much interaction your posts have gotten, as well as how many people they have reached. You can see how your followers have grown over time as well,

---

[1]Launch Digital Marketing. "UTM Codes to Track All of Your Marketing Campaigns." launchdigitalmarketing.com/what-are-utm-codes, (accessed January 17, 2020).

telling you if what you are doing is still drawing in new followers or whether you need to boost your outreach efforts.

On websites like Quora, you can use the data in Quora Ads Manager to help inform you so your ads can be as effective as possible. You can also measure the competitiveness of your ads.[2]

If all this sounds too complicated to manage across multiple social media platforms, and you're looking to simplify and strategize your social media presence and advertising for consistency, you may want to consider using a comprehensive software tool.

Use Comprehensive Software Tools

If you're new to the world of social media marketing, you'll quickly discover a wealth of resources available to make your job easier. These comprehensive software tools help build engagement, allow you to preschedule posts, and even suggest targeted hashtags to use on your social posts.

The available tools make it so much easier to manage your social media. Instead of having to log into various platforms one at a time, you can have it all in one place. These resources can also shorten your learning curve, making it easier to come up with professional hashtags, graphics, and even times for you to post your content that will be best for your customer base.

We have several favorite tools, and they all offer something a bit different in terms of what they do and how they help.

1. *Buffer*: Buffer is a scheduling tool that has been a godsend when it comes to arranging business-focused posts. Buffer does offer a free version that lets you connect as many as three Twitter, Facebook, Pinterest, LinkedIn, or Instagram accounts; however, it will not include the other benefits that come with a paid account. Buffer provides analytics on your past posts, as well as suggested times to post based on when your customers are more likely to be on social media. One of the most significant benefits Buffer offers is the ability to post directly to Instagram business accounts. It can also offer direct scheduling to Pinterest.

---

[2]"Quora for Business." quora.com/business, (accessed January 10, 2020).

2. *Hootsuite*: Hootsuite is one of the prime social media management dashboards. It allows you to connect several accounts at once, and you can post to all major social media platforms. Hootsuite goes beyond scheduling by allowing you to interact with the posts you have published. For example, you can arrange your dashboard into customized columns that allow you to see everything from replies to retweets to upcoming posts all on one screen. If someone likes or responds to your post, you can reply to them directly through the dashboard without ever leaving Hootsuite. You can even use Hootsuite to keep track of specific hashtags. Hootsuite's built-in analytics are also among the best of the bunch.

3. *Creator Studio via Facebook*: Recently, Facebook rolled out a social media scheduling tool called Creator Studio for Facebook and Instagram only. If you connect an Instagram business account to a Facebook page, you can easily schedule posts for the Instagram platform. That gives Creator Studio a significant advantage over many of the other tools on this list, which don't allow direct publishing to Instagram. Since Creator Studio is still in its early stages, it has a few hiccups, but it is a promising piece of software, with the bonus of being free.

4. *Splice*: This video editing tool allows you to combine multiple video clips or edit sections out, making it easier than ever to get in on the idea of video marketing! Videos can attract a lot of attention on social media, and businesses that are using them are likely to see more interaction with what they are posting.

5. *AdEspresso*: Facebook's native ad manager isn't as user-friendly as it could be, especially if you're new to the world of Facebook advertising. Enter AdEspresso, a product of Hootsuite that makes it much easier to ensure you are hitting your target demographic with the ads that you are placing on Facebook. AdEspresso is so easy to use that you can create and place ads and new variations of them in a snap. It also has built-in analytics, so you can track the performance of your ads over time.

6. *Sprout Social*: This all-in-one software tool makes it a breeze to schedule posts, view how these posts are performing, and find the latest trends to post about to stay relevant on social feeds. It offers

several functions that make it easy to control how you use social media marketing in any capacity.

7. *Mailchimp*: This software is all about putting your customers at the center. It has drag-and-drop functionality for creating e-mail marketing campaigns, landing pages, and so much more, so your business can always be current in the world of social media.

8. *HashtagsForLikes*: This web-based software provides you with a list of popular hashtags related to the niche you are in. It can be a great way to gain attention via Instagram or Twitter, where hashtags reign supreme!

9. *Constant Contact*: This user-friendly e-mail campaign software offers adjustable templates you can use to keep your branding on target. It allows you to build e-mail lists and even segment them for various e-mail campaigns you may send throughout the year.

10. *Canva*: While this tool is primarily for graphic design, it can help you ramp up your social media efforts. Because it is so straightforward to use, even people with little to no design experience will find they can create a clean-looking branded graphic to share on social media and help spread the message they want to send to the world.

The tools listed merely scratch the surface of comprehensive social media software tools. As you dig in and do your homework, you'll find an abundance of these available. Some offer free trial versions, while others require monthly or annual fees to use. The secret is finding the right software that fits not only your budget, but your expertise level too.

Those who are just getting started may find it helpful to experiment with a few software tools to find the one that suits them best. Remember to consider functionality, reliability, flexibility, and how you prefer to schedule posts to social platforms. What works for one person may not work for another, and you might play around with a top-of-the-line, highly recommended tool and find it's not a good fit for you. The realm of social media tools is so diverse that everyone can use their best judgment to find the one that suits their needs and experience level.

Chapter 3: Key Takeaways

After reading this chapter, what should you understand?

1. If you're just getting started with social media, focus on one platform at a time to avoid taking on too much at once.
2. Cultivate an audience by starting with current customers.
3. Develop a strategy, and be intentional with what you post.
4. Use built-in analytics to determine if your posts are performing well, and adjust your strategy accordingly.
5. There are many useful tools to shorten the learning curve of social media and make it easier for you to manage. Take advantage of these to post like a pro.

CHAPTER 4

Make It Visual

Social media is a highly visual medium. When you log in to any social media platform, what attracts your attention first: a good graphic or a ton of text? If you're leaning toward graphics, you're not alone. Attention spans are always getting shorter, and there's an increasing number of brands shouting, "Look at me!" An eye-catching graphic can make all the difference when you're trying to build your brand's presence on social media.

Why Focus on Visuals?

The stats speak for themselves. The Brain Rule Rundown (http://www .brainrules.net/vision) states that people remember only about 10 percent of what they hear 3 days later. However, when you add a picture to this, they remember 65 percent of the information. When you understand how much of a punch a visual can pack, your choice is clear: Use graphics whenever possible.

The Essential Aspects of Creating a Graphic

When it comes to any visual you post, try to keep several things in mind. After all, you want to ensure any graphic you post is eye-catching for the right reasons—not one that makes you the laughingstock of the Internet.

- *Make your logo a prominent part of at least some of the graphics you post.* Your logo doesn't have to be on everything if you don't want it to be. However, when you are trying to establish a foothold for your brand, your logo is one of the best tools you have. Remember, someone might share a graphic separately from your post, so it's crucial to include your logo whenever possible.

- *Choose photos wisely.* Never use photos without permission, as doing so can land you in legal hot water. Luckily, there are plenty of sources for free, high-quality images that do not require attribution when used on social media. Later in this chapter, we'll give you resources for these photos.
- *Is your message easy to see?* Although a good graphic is an ideal way to attract attention, you need to avoid using so much text that it's overwhelming or distracting. Less is more when it comes to combining text with graphics.
- *What does your target audience respond to?* It's unlikely you'll hit upon a winning formula for the most engaging graphics right away. There's always a trial-and-error period, where you will need to monitor whether people are interacting with your visual posts, and change them up if need be.

For those who are new to social media, you can easily create designs on your own, as you will see in the following subsections. Check out the following graphic, which shows a clean, straightforward way to communicate heartfelt messages through graphics (Figure 4.1).

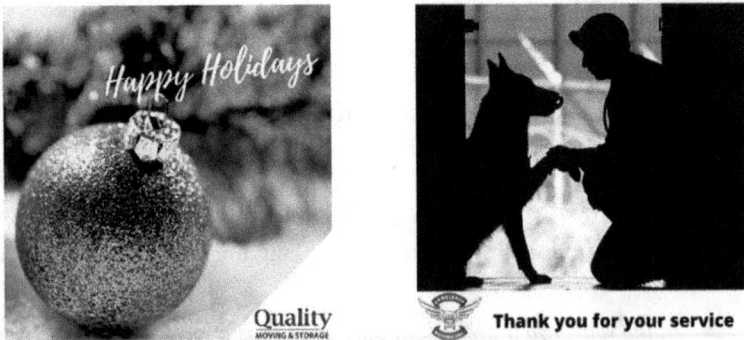

Figure 4.1 Simple graphics that communicate a heartfelt message for your brand

How to Create a Graphic
(Even If You Aren't a Designer)

Good news: You don't need a degree in graphic design to create eye-catching, impactful visuals. Consider some of the photos you have seen on platforms like Instagram, Twitter, and Facebook. In most cases, these were probably quick snapshots taken with a cell phone camera.

For businesses, posting photos that tell the inside story of what's going on in the day-to-day life of your company can be one of the easiest ways to gain attention with a visual and start to build that personal relationship with your followers.

This moving company graphic shows the newest additions to their fleet of trucks (Figure 4.2).

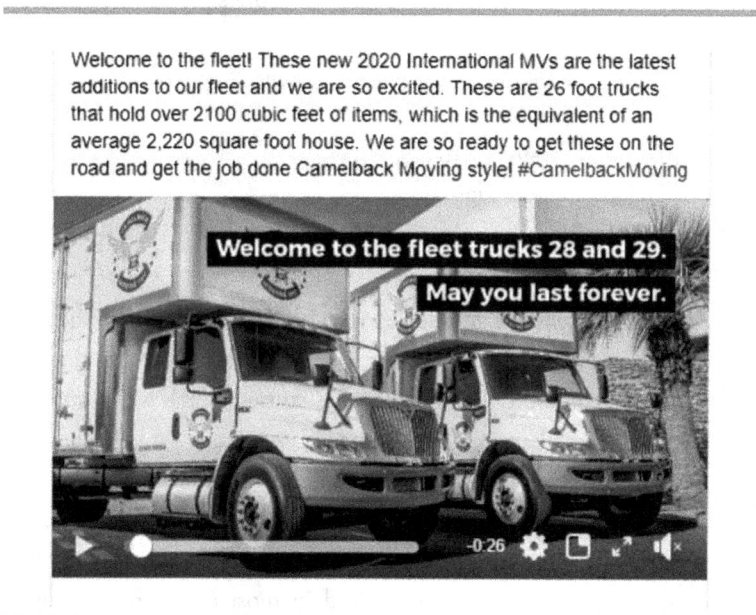

Welcome to the fleet! These new 2020 International MVs are the latest additions to our fleet and we are so excited. These are 26 foot trucks that hold over 2100 cubic feet of items, which is the equivalent of an average 2,220 square foot house. We are so ready to get these on the road and get the job done Camelback Moving style! #CamelbackMoving

Welcome to the fleet trucks 28 and 29.
May you last forever.

Figure 4.2 Newest addition to the fleet of trucks is a fun post for this moving company

If you're just starting out with visuals, remember these top design tips for beginners.

1. *Look for inspiration.* While you don't want to plagiarize any of the designs you find, look to what other businesses are doing. What do you

like about their graphics? What feels off to you? Make notes about these to give you an idea of where you want to start.

2. *Clarity is king.* There's nothing worse than using an illegible font for your graphics. While you may see people experiment with a lesser used font to stand out, there's a good reason people stick with a few tried-and-true basics like Arial, Helvetica, and Times New Roman: They're easy to read. The best advice is to use the same font family for every graphic you make. You'll probably find lots of variants within each font family, such as "narrow," "bold," and "light." Experiment with what you like, but try to avoid putting more than three different types of fonts into each design you create.

3. *Pay attention to the size of your design.* Specific sizes are ideal for different social media platforms. When you stay within these size ranges, you will find your visuals have an even more significant impact on your audience.

   a. Almost any platform can work well with a generic image size of 800 × 800 pixels.

   b. Instagram: 1080 × 1080 pixels

   c. Facebook: 940 × 788 pixels

   d. Pinterest: 735 × 1102 pixels

   e. Twitter: 1024 × 512 pixels

4. *Make the design clean.* While you may be eager to try out all the tools and nifty elements your graphic software offers, don't use them all in the same graphic. Doing so creates clutter, which is not going to encourage people to share your images.

5. *Don't go overboard with colors.* It can be tempting to create a graphic that includes every color of the rainbow. However, the issue of color goes right along with a clean design. Most professionals keep their designs at two to three colors. And in most cases, they are often either complementary colors, or within the same color family.

6. *Practice makes perfect.* Don't get frustrated if your first design attempts don't make as much of a splash as you thought they would. Like every other discipline, it takes time to build graphic design skills. Even if you have an eye for color and are naturally creative, that doesn't mean you won't have a learning curve. Keep working at it, and you will find success.

Design Examples: What Works, What Doesn't

Check out the design below. Does it look clean and respectable to you? Would you want to share it if you saw it on social media?

Figure 4.3 A graphic that is too complicated created confusion

Figure 4.3 is an example of having too much going on at once in one graphic. The stars at the top could be the primary focal point, or maybe it's the lines. Now, you aren't quite sure where to look. In contrast, check out this toned-down design (Figure 4.4).

By removing the lines, making the background less busy, and selecting only one font, this image looks classy and more likely to belong on the social media page of a business.

Here's an example of a clean, clear Instagram post for a laundromat (Figure 4.5).

The key is moderation with design elements...simple is better

Figure 4.4 *The graphic is simplified to grab attention and communicate your message*

columbiapikelaundry • Follow   ...

columbiapikelaundry Enjoy the weekend without having to worry about laundry...even those swimsuits that get coated with chlorine while playing in the pool. See a swimsuit and think about fun instead of work.

#ColumbiaPikeLaundry #SummerTime #FunInTheSun #Laundry #DCMoms #LaundryService #ArlingtonVA #Rosslyn #Ballston #FallsChurch #Alexandria #ArlingtonMoms #SelfCare #WashandFold

30w

13 likes
AUGUST 1, 2019

Add a comment...   Post

Figure 4.5 *Even a laundromat can have fun on Instagram*

Websites to Bookmark

Thankfully, plenty of websites offer free graphic software. With these, you can take a lot of the guesswork out of creating a stunning graphic.

The time you put into crafting your visuals is going to be rewarding, because it will gain you more attention on your social media pages. Here are some websites you will want to bookmark for your visual creation journey. Free photo sites that don't require you to give credit to the photographer include:

- Pexels.com
- Pixabay.com
- Unsplash.com
- Freeimages.com
- Publicdomainpictures.net
- Stockfreeimages.com
- Burst.com

This list continues to grow, as many photographers put their photos online and invite people to use their work for free. In many cases, these are professional photographers hoping to gain more name recognition for themselves and grow their portfolios, or they are hobbyists looking to share the beauty they have captured.

For those who need easy-to-use graphic software to help create visual content, here are several websites to add to your bookmarks bar.

- *Canva.com*: This leading online software offers both free and paid versions that allow you to design graphics for any social media platform you like. Canva stands out because they offer a variety of layouts that allow you to add your photos, logos, and text in an eye-catching way.
- *Lumen5.com:* This video-creation software can help you transform content you have already written into something visual. For example, you can enter the URL for your latest blog, and then the software creates a video for you to post on social media. The process couldn't be any more straightforward. The website will walk

you through every step, including what pictures to use, which text from the blog to choose, and the music you want to play in the background. The free version allows you to create up to 10 videos per month.

- *PicMonkey.com*: Much like Canva, this software allows you to create a limited number of designs each month without having to pay for a membership. You will find they have a few layouts that help with placement of objects, and even with the colors you need to use.

- *BeFunky.com*: This website allows you to upload your photos, then change or enhance them. It is similar to Photoshop, but is much more accessible for beginners to use. You can make photo collages, highlight specific elements of the photo, or even turn a picture into a cartoon.

- *PiktoChart.com*: This graphic design website can help you create infographics. Infographics are an excellent way to create a stunning, social-media-ready visual that also contains valuable information. With several layouts to choose from, PiktoChart makes it a breeze to click and type.

Ideas for Your Visuals

What should you use to create a visual? There are several ways you can integrate visuals into your content marketing plan for social media.

1. *Create graphics with holiday wishes.* Use major holidays like Thanksgiving to inspire your visual creations.
2. *Make attention-grabbing announcements.* Whether you are having a sale or welcoming a new employee on board, make it more special with a graphic.
3. *Make your business come to life.* Remember the moving company that added a truck to its fleet? You can make the everyday happenings of your business into a great story for your company.
4. *Turn statistics into visuals.* Keep in mind that people are more likely to remember information presented to them in a visual format.

5. *Take action shots of your employees at work.* Your customers and potential customers want a good look at who your company is on the inside. Photos are an excellent way to share that.

6. *Create infographics.* These visuals position you as a knowledge leader in your industry. They go a long way in helping show you are the professional to turn to.

These ideas are only the tip of the iceberg. If you have an idea for something you think would make a great visual, give it a shot. The worst-case scenario is that the graphic doesn't turn out the way you hoped, in which case you can scrap it before sharing it on any social platform.

The overall goal of going visual on social media is to make a statement and help your business be more memorable to your customers. In the carefully succinct world of social media, it is worthwhile to put up a picture that speaks a thousand words.

Chapter 4: Key Takeaways

After reading this chapter, what should you understand?

1. Use graphics to grab users' attention, maximize the impact of what you post, and help you stand out in the crowded landscape of social media.

2. You don't need a degree in design to create clean, professional-looking graphics. Plenty of websites offer free software to help with this.

3. Experiment with posting different types of visuals, and see what resonates best with your audience.

CHAPTER 5

Facebook

In our social media work with businesses, we have seen the most success on Facebook. Facebook has the biggest reach of any other platform, with more than 2 billion monthly active users from all over the world. The stats reinforce what we're saying. Facebook remains the top platform for small businesses, with 98 percent of B2C and 89 percent of B2B companies using it to promote their products and services.[1]

Why is Facebook a favorite? Not only is the audience massive, but it also allows for freedoms other social platforms don't necessarily offer. You can opt to share a funny meme to get a few giggles, which would not go over as well on a platform like LinkedIn. You can start a fun poll to get readers involved; you can easily post a simple visual with just a few hashtags; you can share a news article you think your readers would be interested in; and you can even keep things stripped down with a text-only post. The variations of what you can do with Facebook make it incredibly versatile.

The Basics

Setting up your Facebook page is relatively straightforward, but the devil is in the detail. Be sure the description and graphics you use on your Facebook page represent you in the most personable, interesting, and unique way possible. Facebook does a good job of walking you through the setup of your page. We'd like to add a few more tips:

- Make your "About" section pop—it's the first impression you are making with your audience.

---

[1] https://www.viidigital.com/41-facebook-stats-that-matter-to-marketers-in-2019/

- Provide a clear overview of your business that shows the essence of your company's personality and brand.
- Make sure all the details about what you do are accurate and that there aren't any little errors.
- Use easily searchable keywords that define your business.
- Think about your call-to-action buttons and make sure you're using the best one for your business.
- Allow people to leave reviews and make them public so people can see the good work you do.

Get Noticed on Facebook

Whether you've had a business Facebook page for years or are just dipping your toe into these waters, here are helpful tips to keep in mind to get noticed and start to build your audience:

- Reach out to your personal network to encourage them to like your business page.
- Put a prominent link to your Facebook page on your website, as well as in the signature lines of your official company e-mails.
- Highlight customer reviews and work you have done in the past. Be sure to tag your customers in the post so they'll see it.
- E-mail your customer list to ask them to like your Facebook page. Consider any incentives you could offer to encourage them to follow your content.
- Be creative in what you post, and don't forget about offering infographics, free e-books, and webinars to enhance your content.
- Interact with your customers by spreading their content, getting back to them promptly in Messenger, and having fun in the comment sections.
- Share content from other businesses that could refer you to new clients.
- Tag your employees in pictures of what you do each day.
- Post pictures and videos that reflect what you do and are authentic to your brand.
- Use Facebook Live to offer a video tutorial of one of your products or services.

- Run a giveaway or a contest for something that is desirable for most of your customers, and incentivize them to like, share, or comment.

The great thing about Facebook is that you'll find new ways every day to get your name out there. For example, consider this type of post (Figure 5.1).

Are you ready to move out of your parents' house? We can help. #QualityBrawn

Is it time to move out of your parents' house?

Figure 5.1 At the time these former royals were moving out, a moving company made this relevant post

With this meme, a moving company not only used something topical that was at the top of everyone's news feeds, with the duke and duchess of Sussex announcing they were stepping back from their royal responsibilities, but they also used it as an opportunity to highlight their industry. It showcases their humor but also that they are a professional moving company that can help if you emulate the royals and move away from home.

Grow Your Audience

Once you have started developing a following, how can you continue to develop it organically? It's essential to be strategic to develop a following. There is no purpose in having a large audience if they aren't engaging with your posts or if there is no chance of them becoming customers in the future.

If you have not defined your ideal target audience(s), now is an excellent time to start. We had talked before about identifying your target audience, and it's relevant to think of that again as you look to grow your audience on Facebook. Ask yourself questions such as the following:

- What is the average age of your customers?
- Is your audience mostly male, mostly female, or mixed genders?
- What problem does your product or service solve for your customers?
- What geographic area do most of your customers live in?
- Is your product or service transactional in nature, or does it fulfill a lifestyle interest?
- What groups of people are interested in your product or service?
- What kind of hobbies are people into who like your business?

With these questions answered, you continue to know your audience. For example, if you know that you are targeting homeowners who need professional plumbing services, you'll have a good idea of what is going to catch these customers' eyes when you are posting content on Facebook. Would a 30-something couple with two young children be interested in reading an article on how to clean a bathroom when you have roommates? Probably not. They are going to be more interested in an article that outlines what happens when kids flush their toys down the toilet.

Knowing your audience is the secret to *growing* the audience! Otherwise, you may see a few likes on your page, but there's no guarantee they'll be interested in using your services or products.

Post Compelling Content

Another way to attract and retain a large following on Facebook is to share content that resonates with people or provides them with some kind of value. Everything you post should educate, inform, or entertain your audience members. Don't waste people's time or insult their intelligence with boring or irrelevant information.

Imagine you are at a party and somehow you end up stuck in a conversation with another guest who only seems to know how to talk about himself. He rambles on and on, loving the sound of his voice and barely letting you get a word in edgewise. When you do finally get a chance to speak up, the other guest doesn't show any signs of listening to you or being interested in what you have to say. Would you remain in that conversation all night? Chances are good you'd be looking for a way to get out as quickly as possible.

Now, picture yourself at the same party, but instead of talking to a crashing bore, you get lucky and meet someone interesting. This person is an excellent conversationalist who always has a witty remark or exciting story to share and takes time to stop and ask you what you think or if you have ever been in the same situation. You'd probably enjoy your time with that person and may even make plans to meet up with them again in the future.

Think about sharing content on social media as if you are a good party guest. Your goal should be not only to keep the conversation going with funny anecdotes or thought-provoking questions, but also to ask your audience to respond with stories of their own. Don't always talk about yourself or make every post a sales pitch. On Facebook, just as in real life, nobody is interested in people who seem self-centered.

Remember, the word we use most often when we talk about publishing content on Facebook is *sharing*. People who share are generous and open-minded, not rude or conceited. Keeping that in mind, here are some ideas for Facebook content your audience will find valuable:

- Industry infographics, whitepapers, e-books, or videos
- Blog posts that are relevant to your customers' needs or problems
- Entertaining content such as a joke or a meme that pertains to your industry
- Content from other local (noncompetitor) businesses
- Positive news stories about the city or region where you do business
- Photos of your employees interacting with customers or volunteering in the community. These show a more personal and relatable side of your business, instead of trying to promote your products or services (Figure 5.2).

We are so excited to announce that we completed our Christmas tree delivery to the Children's Hospital of Alabama last week! Every year, we help get this done to bring a smile to some kids' faces when these beautiful trees are put up in the hospital. #ChangingSpacesMoving

Figure 5.2 A Christmas tree delivery makes people smile

- Entertaining content such as a joke, meme, or even conducting a poll like the example below. While it does not relate to the business at all, it is fun, and anyone who sees it can vote (Figure 5.3)!

Is it bad luck to take down your holiday decorations before the new year begins? Weigh in with your opinion! #ChangingSpacesMoving

25% Yes, it is bad luck.   75% No, it's not bad luck.

Figure 5.3 A poll on Facebook helps people connect and interact

- Content from other local (noncompetitor) businesses, such as the example below, in which the movers not only tagged the company that provided them with service, but also included a website link for the other local business. It's an excellent way to build goodwill within the community (Figure 5.4).

Camelback Moving · Phoenix AZ Movers   •••
Published by Buffer [?] · January 14 at 2:11 PM · 🌐

We want to give a huge thank you to Derek with Arcadia Signarama for this fabricated piece for our office. We absolutely love it! Signarama
https://buff.ly/2QSSpoD #CamelbackMoving

Figure 5.4 You can build goodwill with partners by posting about them with a link

When posting, include graphics wherever you can. Photos, videos, and even GIFs are inherently eye-catching and can make a world of difference between content people click on and engage with and information they overlook (review Chapter 4 for more details on creating professional-looking visuals, even without a design background).

Also, consider the times of day your target audience is most likely to be online. For example, if you notice you are getting markedly more engagement on content you share in the afternoon than you do in the morning, it makes more sense for you to prioritize publishing your most educational or impactful information after lunch, when people are most likely to see it.

By the same token, try not to undershare or overshare. If you post only once a week, your audience might forget about you, but if you are posting 10 times a day, you might annoy people who assume you are desperate for attention. It may take you some trial and error to find the "sweet spot" for how frequently to post, but let your audience response and reaction be your guide.

In our experience writing for local businesses, we've found the sweet spot seems to be around three posts each week, during the middle of the day and during the weekdays.

How to Advertise on Facebook

Once you have established a business page on Facebook, you will start noticing ways to advertise it. The strength of Facebook advertising lies in its versatility and the exceptional degree of customization it offers. Facebook allows users to target almost any audience in an assortment of placements—both on and off the platform—in a variety of ad formats (Figure 5.5).

Figure 5.5 Facebook advertising is a great way to expand your business page's audience

Crucial questions to ask yourself before you begin include:

- Is it worthwhile spending money on Facebook?
- What is the difference between a Facebook ad and a Facebook post you pay to boost?
- Do you have to be a marketing expert to succeed at Facebook advertising?

The breadth of advertising options Facebook offers doesn't do much if you don't take the time to figure out how to make it work for you. If you've never advertised on Facebook, don't be intimidated. It's more straightforward than you might think. Here are some basic tips to keep in mind as you get started.

1. *Begin with a low advertising budget.* It's better to cap your initial advertising at a budget of $5 or $10 per week, rather than wasting hundreds on advertising nobody responds to. Start slowly with advertising.
2. *Use graphics, but don't put too much text on them.* Most Facebook-approved ads have graphics with minimal text overlays. If you go overboard with text on the graphic, Facebook might not approve the ad, or it will perform poorly.
3. *When in doubt, do your homework.* You'll find a community of helpful Facebook users who will be happy to answer your questions and give you their advice on what has worked and not worked for them.

No matter what your current objectives are, Facebook advertising can bring a strong return on investment. Here are some additional do's and don'ts to keep in mind as you move forward.

1. *Video is a vital marketing tool*—especially when creating ads people will want to interact with. Videos give you more flexibility in how you present your message and pack a visual punch that text-only ads can't hope to match.
2. *Create multiple sets of ad copy.* Focus on the same message with each set of ads, but experiment with different tones. You can use

Facebook's split-testing feature to determine what your audience responds to best.

3. *Don't pay for likes and follows on your page.* There are "black-hat" techniques and options that can negatively affect your business, and we don't suggest using them. You can run an advertising campaign through Facebook to continue to attract new likes on your page through targeting.

4. *Choose how you want to reach users.* You have several options to reach users and attract likes, both on and off Facebook, including Instagram and the audience network. You can also decide if you'd prefer to have your ads appear on desktop, mobile, or both.

5. *Create lookalike audiences.* You probably have some clients that bring higher value than others. Create a custom audience of these users, and then use it to make a lookalike audience. Looking for potential customers who are like the high-value clients you already have presents an irreplaceable opportunity to find more of the customers who are valuable to your business.

So, is Facebook advertising worth your money? Advertising with Facebook allows you to get highly targeted, which is a boon if you are trying to grow your reach, but you need to be smart about it. Start small and experiment to find what works best for your business. If you want to post an ad, create one, and don't forget to check back on it periodically.

If you see an ad you posted is performing exceptionally well, boost it to see even better results. If a post is garnering high engagement, don't be afraid to boost it to expand its reach to a broader audience. Facebook offers these relatively affordable tools to help people reach a broader audience, and you can take advantage of them with a disciplined approach.

Chapter 5: Key Takeaways

After reading this chapter, what should you understand?

1. Facebook is still the world's largest social platform, with 2 billion monthly active users worldwide.

2. Facebook is highly versatile and allows for many different types of posts.

3. Take time to get to know your audience, so you can share the content that's most relevant and engaging.

4. Don't make every post a sales pitch. Mix it up with content that shows a more personable side of your business. Use graphics wherever possible.

5. It may take some trial and error to find the ideal times of day and frequency to post content.

6. You can create Facebook ads to get highly targeted with your audience. Facebook advertising doesn't have to be expensive. You can reach hundreds of people for a few dollars per day.

CHAPTER 6

Instagram and Pinterest

Now, we turn our attention to two social media platforms that are incredibly visual in nature. While most business owners know they need to focus their time and energy on powerhouse platforms like Twitter and Facebook, they often forget about the lighthearted, visual-based apps of Instagram and Pinterest. Don't let the fun, hobby-focused natures of these two platforms fool you—for the right businesses, they are crucial (Figure 6.1).

Figure 6.1 The visual nature of Instagram and Pinterest can be great for business

Why Consider Instagram and Pinterest?

We have combined Instagram and Pinterest in this chapter because they are two of the most visual platforms, but we should note that most of our clients prefer Instagram to Pinterest. Instagram has more than 1 billion active user accounts worldwide every month.[1] Meanwhile, as of the second

---

[1]https://business.instagram.com, (accessed October 20, 2019).

quarter of 2019, Pinterest reports 300 million[2] monthly active users around the globe. Imagine, then, how much your potential for reaching people increases when you establish a presence on these platforms.

In addition, both these websites rely on visuals. And, as we mentioned in Chapter 4, studies have shown[3] that people respond and remember visuals better than they do text. Therefore, Instagram and Pinterest are two easy ways to build your brand's recognition to a broad audience.

The Ins and Outs of Instagram

Most people assume Instagram is straightforward to use, and they are mostly correct. However, using Instagram well requires more than posting a picture you have taken and hoping for the best. Here are tips and tricks you can use to make your posts easy to find and irresistible to share.

1. *Start with the right size.* Believe it or not, the size of the image you post will make a significant difference. The good news is that the Instagram app will automatically scale your photo for you. However, if the graphic you've designed is too large, you run the risk of the app cutting off part of the image. The recommended size for an Instagram image is 1080 × 1080 pixels.

2. *Connect your Facebook account with your Instagram account.* Facebook acquired Instagram in 2012. If you have a presence on both apps, connecting the two accounts can help you cultivate a larger following by making it easier for your current Facebook followers to find you on Instagram.

3. *Use the About section on Instagram to make a statement.* Don't let this section be a repeat of the information anyone can already find on your website. Be more creative with the About section on Instagram. If Facebook represents your older, more conservative aunt or uncle, Instagram is your Bohemian friend who likes their life to be carefree,

---

[2] J. Clement. "Number of Monthly Active Pinterest Users Worldwide from 1st Quarter 2016 to 2nd Quarter 2019 (in Millions)." statista.com/statistics/463353/pinterest-global-mau, (accessed October 20, 2019).

[3] Pixelo. 2018. "Visuals vs. Text: Which Content Format Is Better, and Why?" pixelo.net/visuals-vs-text-content-format-better, (accessed October 20, 2019).

cool, and fun. Try to include keywords relevant to your industry. For example, a moving company in Atlanta would want to include a key phrase like "movers in Atlanta." Meanwhile, an e-commerce company that sells women's clothes will want to include keywords like "women's fashion," "fashionista," etc. The idea is to be creative, while still making it clear who you are.

4. *Be engaged while using Instagram.* Don't merely post your pictures and call it a day. You need to like and comment on other people's photos, and follow those who follow you. The more engaged you are on this platform, the better your results will be.

5. *Use hashtags strategically.* As we will explain in more detail later in this chapter, the right hashtags can be vital to helping boost your Instagram post. It may require some research on your part to get this right, but it's well worth it.

6. *Post compelling visuals.* Even a simple picture of an office can be memorable when combined with the right content and hashtags.

7. *Have fun with it.* Nobody wants to see an Instagram account focused solely on sales. Let your customers see the personal side of your business. Consider posting pictures of your employees' furry friends, or take snapshots of them volunteering within your community.

8. *Find the right time to post your content.* Even the best content will go unseen if you post it at a time when your audience isn't paying attention. Play around with posting at peak times such as lunchtime (11 a.m. to 1 p.m.) and later in the evening (7 to 9 p.m.). Post at different times of the day, and notice how this changes engagements.

9. *Be flexible in how you post to Instagram.* Although there are ways to preschedule posts for each week, you will find some businesses that choose to flood their Instagram pages with tons of images are not doing any better than those who post three times a week. In many cases, overposting can even cause you to lose followers. People should have the impression that you post on Instagram because you want to and not because you are trying to market to them 24/7.

10. *Don't forget the video function of Instagram.* As we'll discuss in more detail in Chapter 8, video content is drawing more eyes than ever before, and you ignore it at your peril. One idea is to invite your customers to provide video testimonials for your Instagram page. This

strategy is an easy way to involve your customers and show them how much you value their business.

11. *Use the Stories functionality on Instagram.* You can have a lot of fun posting to the Stories section of Instagram. The story will only be up for 24 hours, but you can use video, pictures, emoji, fun words, and more to bring even the most mundane office activity to life (Figure 6.2).

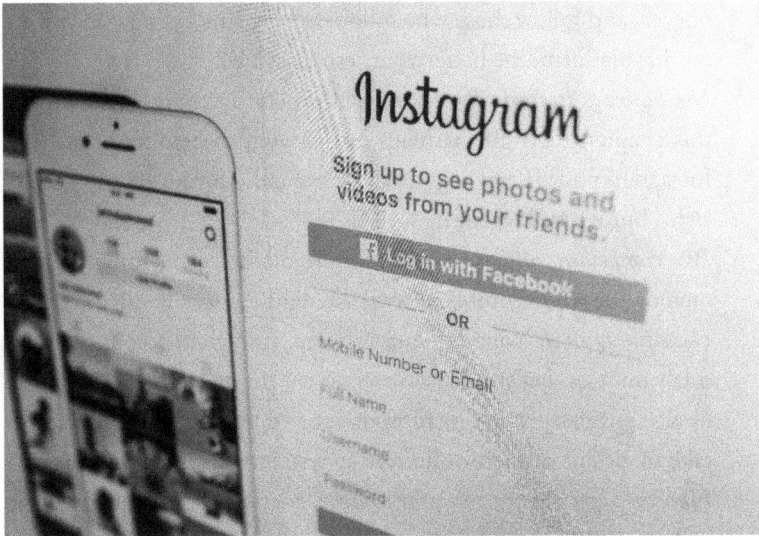

Figure 6.2 Don't miss out on Instagram's Stories feature

Using Hashtags on Instagram

You may already know that the concept of hashtags originated on Twitter. However, it quickly spread to all the other social platforms, and Instagram is where hashtags truly shine. The value of hashtags is that they make it easy for users to find content on specific topics. You can also create unique hashtags for your business—for example, if you have a motto or tagline, you can turn that into a hashtag you use consistently on every post. Here are some ideas for implementing hashtags successfully.

1. *Look to your competition.* What hashtags are they using on their Instagram posts? Use these posts for ideas and for some friendly competition to make sure that yours are better.

2. *Create hashtags for your brand.* There's nothing wrong with using hashtags that are popular in your industry or community, but don't be afraid to throw in a few that are specific to your business, as well. Custom hashtags are an excellent way to create a following for your company.

3. *Don't try to "hijack" a trending hashtag if you don't know what it means.* There's no dearth of horror stories about companies that have fallen victim to jumping aboard with a trending hashtag, then having it backfire. For example, in 2011, at the height of the Arab Spring, designer Kenneth Cole posted a tone-deaf tweet using the hashtag #Cairo to promote his new spring collection. Predictably, there was a swift online backlash[4] to the hashtag, forcing Cole to delete the tweet and issue an apology. Remember, the Internet doesn't forget, and screenshots live forever. The results of incorrect hashtag use are often detrimental to the brand, and your business might not be able to bounce back from your mistake.

4. *Use hashtags strategically.* While Instagram allows you to use up to 30 hashtags on a single post, there's no need to go overboard every time you post something. One study, by TrackMaven, found posts with nine hashtags[5] get the most engagement, but you may have to experiment to find your sweet spot.

Should You Brand Your Images?

Should you brand the images you are posting on social media? The answers are both yes and no. If you want your company's image to be fun and lighthearted, avoid branding every image you post. Instead, brand a few posts and leave others the way you uploaded them. Branding every

---

[4]B. Ehrlich. 2011. "Kenneth Cole's #Cairo Tweet Angers the Internet." mashable.com/2011/02/03/kenneth-cole-egypt, (accessed October 20, 2019).
[5]R. Fearn. 2019. "How Many Hashtags Should I Use On Instagram In 2019? This Is What the Experts Recommend." bustle.com/p/how-many-hashtags-should-i-use-on-instagram-in-2019-this-is-what-the-experts-recommend-15936290, (accessed October 20, 2019).

post may not be getting you any further to your goals for Instagram marketing.

Also, if you are planning to post any images you did not take, you will need to get the photographer's permission to use them. Refer to Chapter 4 for a list of websites that offer royalty-free images you can use without worrying about copyright issues coming into play.

Pinterest: It's Not Just for Crafts Anymore

If you've never used Pinterest, you might have heard the platform caters solely to women. Although Pinterest's audience does skew heavily female, more men have begun to discover and use the platform as well. In 2018, 50 percent of all new Pinterest user signups were men.[6] Meanwhile, eMarketer predicts Pinterest's audience will have a 70/30 gender split by 2022.[7]

What started as a platform for sharing cute craft ideas and other do-it-yourself (DIY) décor has since branched out. Now, you can find things like marketing ideas, business tips, and graphic design inspiration on Pinterest. It has grown into a legitimate social media site, which is why you might want to consider giving it a place in your marketing strategy.

Learning Pinterest to Help Your Business

Pinterest is slightly different from the other social media platforms, and it may take a bit of time to learn the do's and don'ts. Hopefully, you can use these tips and tricks to turn your Pinterest profile into something that works for you.

1. *Set up a Pinterest business account.* Having a business account provides you with access to analytics and other information to help you see how well your pins are doing.
2. *Use your logo as your Pinterest profile picture.* When people find you on Pinterest, they'll know what to expect from your brand.

---

[6]https://allprowebdesigns.com/2019/02/23-pinterest-statistics-that-matter-to-marketers-in-2019/

[7]R. Kats. 2018. "Who Is Using Pinterest in the U.S.?" emarketer.com/content/the-social-series-who-s-using-pinterest-infographic, (accessed October 20, 2019).

3. *Complete your profile as soon as possible.* Use keywords that relate to your business, and write a brief description of who you are and what you offer the market. Be sure to include your website link in the bio to redirect people there.

4. *Confirm your website when signing up with Pinterest.* Doing so will allow you to pin items directly from your website.

5. *Create your first boards.* Boards are a way to keep the images you pin more organized. When naming these boards, be sure to use keywords that apply to your industry. For example, a marketing company may have boards called "Facebook Marketing Tips" or "How to Brand Your Business on Instagram."

6. *Start developing pins.* Make sure the images you pin are easy to read and provide value. Later in this chapter, we will take a closer look at appropriate visuals and sizes to help you get this set up correctly.

7. *Include your website in the pin.* You can link any image you pin to a blog or specific product page on your website, so take advantage of this feature when posting.

8. *As always, be aware of when you are posting.* Most people look at Pinterest in their downtime during evenings and weekends. While you may be active on your other social media profiles in the middle of the day, try to alter this schedule for Pinterest. The timing of your posts can make a big difference.

Styling Your Pinterest Posts

Because Pinterest is an image-based platform, you want to make sure you're taking time to create posts people are going to want to repin. Thus, it needs to be something of interest to the consumer base. Here are tips for creating a masterpiece of a pin.

1. *Create an image that is longer than it is wide.* The best size for a Pinterest pin is 735 × 1102 pixels. Pinterest posts that are sized appropriately have a better chance of others seeing and sharing your content.

2. *Add content onto the pin if you like.* For example, the size of the graphics on Pinterest naturally lends itself to infographics. The more

worthy the content within the visual Pinterest post, the more likely it is that others will share it.

3. *Consider the image you're posting.* You want the image on Pinterest to be different than what other people in your industry are sharing, which means you may have to do a little bit of research to find what will work.

4. *Post pins that incorporate your logo and color palette.* Remember, the name of the game is to get other people to share what you pin. The more you can get your logo and branding out into the world, the better the results will be for you.

Do You Need Hashtags on Pinterest?

Those who have been following Pinterest may already know that this platform initially restricted the use of hashtags. However, those rules have changed. Now, Pinterest encourages hashtags, and they can be an excellent way to help people find the content you post. Here are some strategies you can use to get started.

1. *Place hashtags at the end of your posts.* Do not sprinkle hashtags throughout your message, as it can be distracting.

2. *Don't go crazy with hashtags.* Pinterest allows users to add up to 20 hashtags on a post, but this may be overkill. Many people are opting for two to eight hashtags on posts.

3. *Search for the right hashtags for your business.* Enter your hashtag phrase into Pinterest's search bar. Make certain any hashtag you use is relevant to your business, products, and services.

4. *Make your branded hashtag first in the list.* If you establish a unique hashtag for your company, it's a best practice to use it on every post, and always make it first if you're posting multiple hashtags.

Whether you decide to incorporate Instagram, Pinterest, or both into your marketing plan, be strategic. Don't post random images that don't make sense for your brand, and always be authentic. If you are smart about your approach, you can find success with these two image-based platforms.

Chapter 6: Key Takeaways

After reading this chapter, what should you understand?

1. Both Instagram and Pinterest are highly visual content platforms, so take advantage of that.
2. Hashtag research is going to be a significant component of your plan for using either of these two platforms successfully.
3. Take time to create eye-catching visuals to post to Instagram and Pinterest, and make sure they are the right sizes so no components get cut off.
4. When posting content, your timing plays a major role in whether people see and interact with your post or whether it goes ignored.

CHAPTER 7

LinkedIn

LinkedIn is one of the oldest social media platforms, having been around since 2002. Despite its venerability, however, LinkedIn can be an underused and misunderstood social network. Most people use LinkedIn as their online résumé and nothing more. However, this professional social media network has much more potential than you probably realize. For example, LinkedIn has built credible authority on Google and other search engines, which your company can use to its advantage. Read on for our top advice on how to market your small business on LinkedIn (Figure 7.1).

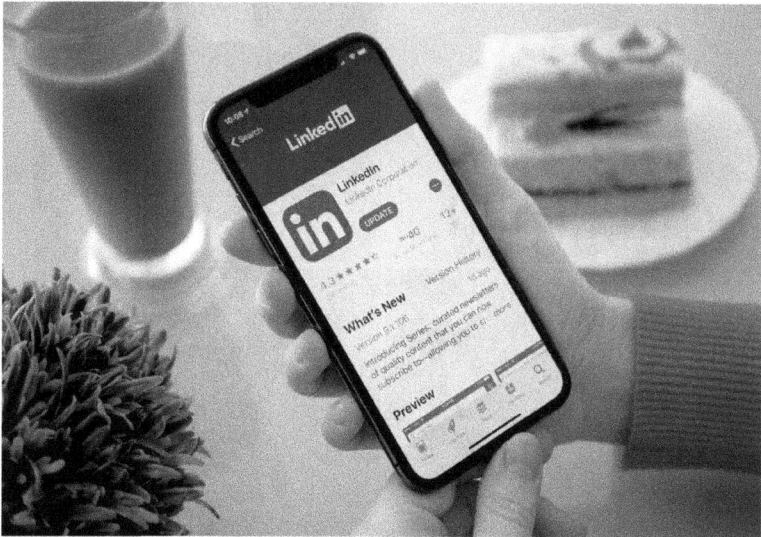

Figure 7.1 LinkedIn is a great tool for local businesses

Polish Your Profile

The first step to marketing success on LinkedIn is to make sure your professional profile is up to date. When people find you on LinkedIn, you want to have a profile that makes you stand out from your competition and that demonstrates why someone should want to work with you.

There are many ways to polish and fine-tune your LinkedIn profile to make it more impressive. Remember to be intentional about the photo you use for your profile. A poorly lit selfie you took at a party or a photo of yourself with other people isn't going to cut it. Make sure the photo accurately represents you and how you want people to perceive you. For an example of which photos are appropriate for different platforms, we can look back on the "Dolly Parton Challenge" that took over the Internet in early 2020. Check out comedian Ellen DeGeneres and her take on the LinkedIn photo (and photos for other platforms, Figure 7.2).

Figure 7.2 Ellen DeGeneres takes on the Dolly Parton Challenge in early 2020

Work on getting your LinkedIn profile as close to 100 percent complete as you can, then fine-tune it over time, adding new skills, awards, endorsements, and outstanding samples of your work. Be sure to optimize your profile as soon as possible—you don't want your ideal client to search for your areas of expertise and find your competition instead.

Use Company Pages to Your Advantage

Once your LinkedIn profile is shipshape and fully up to date, create a company page for your business—if you haven't already done so. Your company's profile on LinkedIn can work to promote your business, what you offer, your employees, and more to prospective customers.

Your next step after developing your company page is to optimize it for search. As we have already mentioned, LinkedIn has amassed an incredible amount of clout on Google, but it is also a powerful search engine in its own right.

Whether your audience is searching on LinkedIn or off, a well-optimized company page can help you gain visibility among people searching for the products or services you provide. Here are three ways to optimize your company page for search.

- *Use keywords in your company profile.* Be sure to choose words and phrases that accurately represent who you are and what you do. If you're not sure how to approach this, think about what words or phrases you use to describe your product or service.
- *Link back to your company page.* These links are vital for boosting your ranking in searches. Be sure there are prominent links to your company page from your website, blog, and other content you publish online. Also, make sure your employees, contractors, and anyone else who works with you links to your company page from their LinkedIn profiles.
- *Share relevant content frequently.* As with other social networks, sharing is crucial to your visibility on LinkedIn. When you publish updates from your company page, they also appear on your public page, allowing Google to index your content. The more frequently you share interesting, engaging updates, the higher your page will appear in search results.

Remember our earlier analogy about the tedious party guest who only wanted to talk about himself? Don't be that person on LinkedIn. Although it can be tempting to use the benefits of your products and services as inspiration for the content you publish on your company page, "sales-y" content is just as much of a turnoff on LinkedIn as it is on other social media platforms.

Instead of using LinkedIn as a continual sales pitch for your company, consider offering advice that helps address people's challenges or pain points or answer some of the most common questions people have about your industry. This strategy will position you as an expert authority in your field. And if you come across someone else's post that makes a relevant point or causes you to nod your head thoughtfully, don't hesitate to share it with your followers.

Connect with People in LinkedIn Groups

LinkedIn might not have the heavyweight status Facebook enjoys, but when it comes to generating leads, its powerful reach is nothing to scoff at. Consider the results of one HubSpot study, which suggests LinkedIn is a whopping 277 percent more effective for lead generation than Facebook and Twitter.[1]

The people who find value in LinkedIn are professional decision-makers who are looking to make long-lasting business relationships. For these people, LinkedIn groups are the closest online equivalent to traditional in-person networking meetups and events.

Groups can give you access to people and discussions related to an industry, topic, or even geographic region. Learning how to use this feature of LinkedIn effectively is a sound strategy for building a network and generating viable leads.

Of course, one way to use LinkedIn groups is to join a few that are relevant to your field or areas of expertise. For example, if you are a financial

---

[1]R. Corliss. 2012. "LinkedIn 277% More Effective for Lead Generation Than Facebook & Twitter." blog.hubspot.com/blog/tabid/6307/bid/30030/linkedin-277-more-effective-for-lead-generation-than-facebook-twitter-new-data.aspx, (accessed June 30, 2019).

advisor, the group called Finance Club has more than 930,000 members as of the time of this writing. Or if you offer consulting services, you can join the Consultants Network group, which has more than 465,000 members worldwide. If only a fraction of a fraction of those group members turned out to be qualified leads for you, it would still be worth your time to participate in groups like these.

To get started participating in LinkedIn groups, review what others have posted and add relevant replies to strike up conversations. Since the replies you post are publicly available to all group members, you can use this technique to prove your expertise about a given topic.

Once you get the hang of LinkedIn groups, starting one of your own can be a valuable strategy for growing your network online. Consider a topic your current and future customers—and even your competitors— might find interesting, and form a group around it. A word of caution, however: Do not start a group if you're not prepared to spend the time and energy nurturing it by posting content updates and moderating and encouraging group participation. Never start a group intending to use it for self-promotion, and don't let other members of the group post that kind of content, either.

How to Advertise on LinkedIn

There are two broad categories of LinkedIn advertising: sponsored content and advertising campaigns. Here's our breakdown of how to use both to your advantage when marketing your business.

When you publish something on LinkedIn that your target audience finds particularly valuable or engaging, consider "sponsoring" it, which allows you to promote your content directly to the LinkedIn feeds of the connections you want to reach on LinkedIn. This tactic will help you gain new LinkedIn followers by ensuring more people are seeing the updates you post.

Along with sponsored posts, LinkedIn offers two additional ways to advertise: self-service ads and managed campaigns. LinkedIn allows you to set a daily spending cap of as little as $2 per day. You can also choose whether you would prefer to pay based on clicks or impressions. LinkedIn's campaign manager allows you to stop running your ad anytime. Be sure to use LinkedIn's conversion tracking feature to keep up with the leads you're getting from your advertising.

As with Facebook advertising, LinkedIn offers comprehensive targeting options to help you reach your ideal audience with pinpoint accuracy. For example, if you only want C-level executives to see your ad, LinkedIn makes that easy.

Drill Down Deeper with Analytics

How do you create compelling content your audience will respond to? It's easier when you start by understanding their preferences and behaviors. LinkedIn offers several ways to uncover these.

Use the Marketing tab on your company's page to keep track of your analytics, which include reach, engagement, visitor demographics, and more. These analytics will let you know immediately what is and isn't hitting the mark. With that insight, you can shape your campaign around the information and make data-informed decisions that lead to better results.

Chapter 7: Key Takeaways

After reading this chapter, what should you understand?

1. LinkedIn is more than your online résumé. To use it to its fullest, be sure to keep your profile professional-looking and up to date.
2. Because it's been around so long, LinkedIn enjoys considerable authority on Google and is also a powerful search engine on its own.
3. Use the power of LinkedIn groups to generate new leads. Join groups that are relevant to your business, and become part of the conversation. Post articles that demonstrate your expertise.
4. Advertising on LinkedIn is affordable and allows you to target highly specific groups.

CHAPTER 8

YouTube

Since its launch in 2005, the video-sharing platform YouTube has become an indispensable advertising and marketing tool for businesses in every industry, of every size, to promote their products to prospects and customers. The scope of this website is undeniable—its 1.9 billion monthly users have made it the world's second-largest search engine after Google.[1] But how can you tap into that massive audience and use it to market your business (Figure 8.1)?

Figure 8.1 YouTube is everywhere

---

[1] F. Baird. 2019. "The Complete Guide to YouTube Ads for Marketers." blog.hootsuite.com/youtube-advertising, (accessed July 6, 2019).

The good news is that just about every type of business can learn to use YouTube effectively, including B2B and B2C companies of any size, as well as freelancers, consultants, and solopreneurs who have valuable expertise to share. Since anyone can upload a video to YouTube at no cost, it is also one of the most affordable platforms for businesses on a tight marketing budget.

What Makes Video Content So Effective?

If video isn't already part of your marketing strategy, consider these compelling statistics about its popularity and value:

- People watch more than 500 million hours of videos on YouTube each day.
- The average user spends 88 percent more time on a website with video.
- Viewers retain 95 percent of a message when they watch it in a video, compared with only 10 percent when reading it in text.[2]

These three facts alone should be more than enough to convince you of the value of video and why most users find it so engaging. If you aren't already using YouTube to market your business, you could be missing out on valuable opportunities to connect with new audiences and promote your products or services to new, qualified leads. But where should you begin?

Getting Started with YouTube Marketing

The idea of filming and posting videos may sound intimidating, but it's more straightforward than you might think to use YouTube to market your business. The secret is to start with a strategy that ensures people will find, watch, and act on your video content.

---

[2] T.J. McCue. 2018. "Video Marketing in 2018 Continues to Explode as Way to Reach Customers." forbes.com/sites/tjmccue/2018/06/22/video-marketing-2018-trends-continues-to-explode-as-the-way-to-reach-customers, (accessed July 6, 2019).

Step 1: Figure Out Your Format

You can create an effective marketing video in a variety of ways. Specific styles work better for some niches than others. You'll also find that some will resonate more with your audience. Check out the list of formats below and experiment with different ones to determine which works best for your business.

- Talking head
- Interview
- Screenshare (in which you film what you're doing on a computer screen)
- How-to, tutorial, or explainer
- Video blog
- Product review
- If you have a brick-and-mortar business, consider uploading videos shot in the style of a TV commercial.

Step 2: Create Your Videos

One of the qualities that makes YouTube marketing so accessible is that you don't need to invest a lot of money in expensive equipment to create and upload your videos. You could even use your smartphone to film the whole thing. Make sure the area you're filming in is well lit, so viewers can see everything. Also, your sound quality should be decent and not muffled—that's one reason you might want to invest in a microphone at some point.

Consider using a tripod to keep the camera steady, too. You can then use some straightforward video editing software to add titles and edit any mistakes or switch between different shots. There are several free video editing programs available online.

When creating videos, take your audience's attention span into account. Often, shorter videos work better for sharing on social media. Experiment with different lengths and see what works best for your audience. For a quick video, beyond something that is knowingly instructional, we recommend anything that is shorter than 1½ minutes, and ideally it is around 45 seconds.

Step 3: Use Keywords Strategically

Keywords are phrases that describe what your video is about and help people find you. For example, if you're selling an online cooking class, some keywords could be "how to cook" or "home chef." You will put those keywords in your video title, the description, and tags. Using keywords is smart because they tell YouTube's search feature what the content of the video is. When people search for videos like yours, they won't struggle to find them.

You can use Google's keyword tool to find keywords in your industry segment that get a lot of searches. You should also check out videos from your competitors and be sure to use the same keywords as they do.

Step 4: Include Effective Calls to Action

The whole point of investing time and effort into creating YouTube videos is to attract viewers who then take an action that gets them closer to becoming your customer. Usually, people who market on YouTube aren't using their videos to directly sell their product or service. Instead, they're generating leads they can continually market to.

In your video description, you should include a link to your website, blog, or landing page. At the end of your video, you should also include a call to action that encourages people to learn more, ideally on your website. Wherever you direct your viewers, be sure you have a way to capture their contact information, like a website address. Some other calls to action include asking them to rate your video, subscribe to your YouTube channel, and follow you on Facebook, Twitter, and other social media. You can also encourage people to share your video with their friends or online followers.

Step 5: Be Social

Remember, YouTube is a social network. That means you should have an active presence. Monitor the comments section of your video so you can thank people for their comments and respond to their questions.

You might also find that leaving constructive feedback on other people's videos is a good way to encourage them to check out your channel.

Another technique is to create playlists of videos on a similar theme or topic. You could include your videos, as well as those that others have posted.

Step 6: Amplify Your Reach

Once you've invested the effort in creating and posting YouTube videos, don't wait for people to stumble across them. Tell the world about your YouTube channel. Spread the word on your blog; embed your videos on your website; share them on Facebook, Twitter, and LinkedIn; or send an e-mail to your subscribers. However you reach out to your current and potential customers, don't miss the opportunity to ask them to check out your YouTube videos.

How to Create Ads on YouTube

Because of YouTube's massive reach, it's also become one of the most sought-after online platforms for advertisers. YouTube takes Google search history into account when serving ads, so when you create ads for YouTube, you're essentially combining the audiences of the two most substantial search engines.

Once you've uploaded your ad footage to YouTube, you'll need to set up a campaign with a targeted audience.

1. Click Campaigns on the main toolbar.
2. Click the +Campaign button, then New Campaign.
3. Select Video as your campaign type.
4. Establish your campaign goal and subtype.
5. Name your campaign.
6. Enter your budget.
7. Enter the locations and networks where you want your ad to appear, as well as the locations and networks you'd like to exclude.
8. Enter your target audience's language.
9. Name your ad group.
10. Establish your bid amounts.
11. Set your target audience.

YouTube ads are low-risk, high-reward and cost-effective. Because they are priced per 1,000 views, it's easy to control how much you spend. Advertising on YouTube is also one of the best ways to gain exposure for your brand and drive engagement on your channel, sometimes by as much as 500 percent.[3]

Chapter 8: Key Takeaways

After reading this chapter, what should you understand?

1. YouTube is free to use and has virtually no barriers to entry, making it an ideal platform for small businesses trying to grow their online brand on a shoestring budget.
2. People find video content engaging and memorable and will spend time watching videos you post, although shorter clips are usually more effective.
3. Be sure to include keywords and calls to action in every video you upload.
4. Share the videos you create on other platforms. Embed them on your website or into e-mails. Post them to LinkedIn, Twitter, and Facebook.
5. Take advantage of YouTube's affordable advertising to generate even more exposure for your brand.

---

[3]H. Blumenstein, C. O'Neal-Hart. "How YouTube Extends the Reach and Engagement of Your Video Advertising." thinkwithgoogle.com/marketing-resources/how-youtube-extends-reach-engagement-of-video-advertising, (accessed September 2, 2019).

CHAPTER 9

Twitter

Twitter users post an average of 500,000 tweets per day.[1] Twitter is a social behemoth connecting people, usually based on the most recent news. How can you jump in and join the conversation—and grow your business while doing so? Here are some of our top Twitter tips (Figure 9.1).

Figure 9.1 Jump in and join the conversation on Twitter

Establish Your Goals

Setting social media goals is necessary for any platform you decide is worth your time. If you don't have clearly defined goals, your posts may end up being sporadic and lack focused content that aligns with your

---

[1]"Twitter Usage Statistics." internetlivestats.com/twitter-statistics, (accessed October 28, 2019).

brand. Choose three goals to spend time on—any more than that, and you'll end up diluting your message.

Examples of common goals for Twitter include the following:

- Posting relevant news articles about your business or industry
- Making your audience aware of the latest trends
- Connecting with decision-makers
- Increasing direct sales
- Supporting customers
- Improving awareness of your brand
- Keeping up with industry trends

Write down your top three goals and determine what metrics you want to track, such as mentions or link clicks. These will come in handy later when you're reviewing your analytics reports.

Join the Hashtag Bandwagon

Of all the social platforms we've discussed here, Twitter is, perhaps, the most in-the-moment tool of them all. According to a 2017 study conducted by Twitter, 54 percent of daily users of the platform question the importance of any breaking news story they can't find on Twitter.[2]

With that in mind, how can you be an influential conversation starter on Twitter? One key is to use hashtags strategically. Though hashtags are now a common sight across all major social media platforms, they originated on Twitter. You can use them to help make your tweets easier for people to find and allow people to keep track of the conversation around a specific topic. Look ahead and plan fun hashtagged tweets around holidays or designated national days such as:

- #NationalPuppyDay—March 23
- #StarWarsDay—May 4
- #NationalChocolateChipCookieDay—August 4

---

[2]C. Stennis. 2018. "Defining What Makes Twitter's Audience Unique." blog.twitter .com/marketing/en_us/topics/research/2018/defining-what-makes-twitters-audience-unique.html, (accessed October 28, 2019).

In addition to piggybacking on trending hashtags, you can start one of your own. For example, if your business hosts an awards show or meetup, consider live-tweeting from the event and adding the hashtag to every tweet to create conversation and excitement around what you're doing. Or you can use hashtags to identify what you do, like an ultra-modern Yellow Pages. For instance, if you are a certified public accountant (CPA) in the Birmingham, AL, area, use hashtags like #TaxPrepBirmingham or #BirminghamTaxPro during tax season to make it easier for people to find your local business.

Follow Influencers

If you're just getting started on establishing your Twitter presence, you're likely wondering what you can do to grow your base of followers. One tactic is to look for people in your community with large Twitter followings, and follow them. When they tweet something that is relevant to your audience, engage with them by liking, replying, or retweeting.

Post a mix of original content and retweets, and try to tweet several times each day. Because of how quickly information moves on Twitter, you'll need to tweet relatively often to ensure people see what you have to say.

You can use a tool such as Buffer or Hootsuite (see Chapter 3) to plan and schedule your tweets in advance so you don't get overwhelmed trying to keep up with content. These "dashboard"-style tools also have built-in analytics to help you stay on top of how well your tweets are performing and what content people are engaging with the most.

Create Lists

Lists are an excellent way to fully reap the benefits of Twitter for your business. Because of the sheer volume of content people are discussing at any given moment, relevant information can be a challenge to find. Curated Twitter lists that you develop and nurture over time serve as a permanent filter for each of your points of interest.

Here's how to create lists on Twitter.

1. Start by going to your Twitter avatar and clicking Lists.
2. In the right-hand sidebar, click Create New List.

3. Name your list, add a description, set the privacy, and save.

4. After you create a list, populate it with the Twitter handles of those who fit into that category.

5. Continue to grow and nurture your lists over time.

Now that you know how to create lists, what are some strategic ways you can use them for your business?

1. *Monitor competitors*: Keep your competitors' Twitter accounts in one handy list, so you can easily check on their activities. See what's working well for them, and use it as inspiration. This is an example of a time when you want to make your Twitter list private. That way, your competitors won't know you are keeping an eye on them.

2. *Connect with industry leaders*: Use a list to manage and improve your relationship with those at the forefront of your industry. Retweet them, and be sure to reply if they ask a question that pertains to your area of expertise. Position yourself as a valuable resource by sharing your list with your Twitter followers.

3. *Stay abreast of trends*: To keep up with the latest news and trends on Twitter without getting distracted by irrelevant tweets, create a list. Add the top users in your industry to one news-oriented Twitter list. Make your list unique by finding up-and-coming bloggers, reporters, and other news sources to add to your list.

4. *Promote events*: If you're planning a large event such as a trade show or a keynote luncheon, create a Twitter list of registered attendees and anyone who will be speaking. People who are interested in your event will appreciate the opportunity to connect ahead of time, and people who can't make it will still feel like they're in the loop.

5. *Help maintain customer service*: Social media has created an entirely new way for companies and customers to interact. Many people would prefer to reach out online and get instant answers than to call a number and end up on hold. Whenever customers mention you on Twitter, add them to your list. That way, they'll all be in one place so that you can interact with their tweets by responding to them and asking them how they're doing.

How to Advertise on Twitter

If you're looking for an affordable and highly targeted advertising medium, Twitter is an excellent resource. Advertising on Twitter enables you to promote individual tweets or entire campaigns dedicated to specific objectives and to put your content in front of selected groups of people who don't follow you yet.

First, decide whether you want to promote your tweets or run Twitter ads. Promoted tweets appear in the streams and search results of specific users, whereas Twitter ads rely on multiple groups of tweets to accomplish a single goal for your brand. Depending on your objective, Twitter ads can display your username in places other than a user's newsfeed, such as the "Who to Follow" section to the right of their Twitter home page.

If your goal is to attract attention, promoted tweets might be exactly what the doctor ordered. With this option, you pay a flat monthly fee for as long as you're promoting a tweet. It's perfect for getting exposure for your business and generating new leads.

If you're looking to grow your follower base or build up your audience by appealing to targeted people, Twitter ads offer a bit more ammunition. When you set up a Twitter ad, you choose from among eight objectives:

- App installs
- Followers
- Tweet engagements
- Promoted video views
- Website clicks or conversions
- App reengagements
- In-stream video views (preroll)
- Awareness

You will also need to determine your ad's start and end dates, as well as your total budget. Throughout each day of your campaign, the daily budget will pay your maximum set amount at intervals you define yourself. You can be highly choosy about the audience you select to see your ads and promoted tweets, and it's smart to take some time to fine-tune your audience, creative, and message for the maximum impact.

Chapter 9: Key Takeaways

After reading this chapter, what should you understand?

1. You can gain a following on Twitter by using hashtags creatively, following and engaging with influencers, and posting several times per day.
2. Use Twitter lists to keep up with competitors, boost your relationships with industry leaders, and stay abreast of trends and news.
3. Twitter offers an excellent way to advertise and attract a larger base of followers. You can also promote specific tweets to get them in front of designated users.

CHAPTER 10

Next-Level Social Media

There's no doubt that social media has been growing and changing. If you want to stay relevant online, you must be adaptable. Sound like a tall order? Learning and evolving can be fun, when you have some direction. Take a trip with us into the future, where the possibilities for social media marketing are endless.

First, we will take you through the social media platforms that are emerging as competitors to the major players we've highlighted in this book. Next, we'll provide an overview of the elements of the present of social media that will be a part of its future, including developments in advertising, microinfluencers, and visual branding. Finally, we'll delve into stories, video content, and augmented reality.

As the possibilities become realities, you will need to ask yourself: *How can I stay relevant by keeping up with these changes?*

Social Media Platforms on the Rise

We all know Facebook has been the leader of the social media pack for some time, but trends show the use of this platform finally starting to slow down. It's still a smart strategy to continue marketing on Facebook, but be aware that other platforms may take the lead in the not-too-distant future.

TikTok is on the rise among the younger demographic (25 years old and younger). NextDoor is a social sharing platform that is hyper-local among communities and neighborhoods. As outlets like these grow their audience numbers and become more relevant as players in this space, advertising on these platforms is just getting started for businesses. We've addressed platforms that have been adding users, like Instagram, YouTube,

Figure 10.1 Stay relevant by keeping up with changes in social media

and LinkedIn. Other growing social media platforms we haven't discussed yet include Snapchat, Quora, and Reddit (Figure 10.1).[1]

LinkedIn, Quora, and Reddit have all grown their advertising capabilities in scope, as there are now multiple options for the types of ads users can create. They have also grown in depth, as technological advances allow businesses to select and adjust their target audiences. It's essential to be on the lookout for new social media platforms. To stay in the know, you can search online to find out which ones you need to pay attention to. Undoubtedly, future editions of this book will look different as more platforms come into play.

One new platform on the rise is TikTok, a visually based and musically integrative app that uses filters.[2] As of this writing, TikTok boasts over 500 million users. Lasso is another one to look out for, as it is similar to TikTok. Facebook, the proven leader among social media platforms,

---

[1]A. Gesenhues. 2019. "Welcome to the Next Era of Social Media Marketing." marketingland.com/welcome-to-the-next-era-of-social-media-marketing-262718, (accessed January 10, 2020).

[2]P. Bump. 2019. "5 New Social Media Platforms Marketers Should Watch in 2020." blog.hubspot.com/marketing/new-social-media, (accessed December 31, 2019).

launched Lasso in November 2018.[3] Another is Caffeine, which provides users with the ability to live-stream video content, something that appeals to younger generations.

In addition to those visually based platforms, LinkedIn has developed its unique approach to ads, as we discussed in Chapter 7. LinkedIn can be an excellent way for customers to find and learn about you, even if you haven't launched a professional website yet. You may want to consider LinkedIn advertising if the product or service you are offering caters to professionals in any way.[4]

Let's revisit the Landscape of Social Media chart we laid out for you at the beginning of the book so you can get another look at where the platforms stand right now and how you can assess whether a new one will work for your business (Figure 10.2).

Quora, an information networking website, has followed shortly behind LinkedIn, developing keyword targeting and other useful tools for those using its advertising space.[5]

Reddit, a social news platform that allows users to upvote and down-vote on posts, has advertising space for a different kind of audience. If your company or product has any political links or implications, this might be a good place to advertise. Basically, there are three steps to advertising on Reddit: Target your audience, tell your story, and measure your success.[6]

Messaging apps have been introduced through Facebook and other social media. WhatsApp, for example, provides a unique way for businesses to connect with customers through a messaging service. Businesses can use WhatsApp to confirm customer information, answer customer questions, and aid customers while they are shopping or checking out.[7]

---

[3]J. Constine, T. Hatmaker. 2018. "Facebook Launches Lasso, Its Music and Video TikTok Clone." techcrunch.com/2018/11/09/lasso-facebook-app-store, (accessed December 31, 2019).

[4]LinkedIn Corporation. "Advertise on LinkedIn." business.linkedin.com/marketing-solutions/ads, (accessed January 10, 2020).

[5]Quora Inc. "Quora Ad Products." go.quoraforbusiness.com/ad-products, (accessed January 10, 2020).

[6]"Advertise on Reddit." reddit.com/adsregister?dest=https://ads.reddit.com, (accessed January 1, 2020).

[7]WhatsApp Inc. "WhatsApp Business App." whatsapp.com/business, (accessed January 10, 2020).

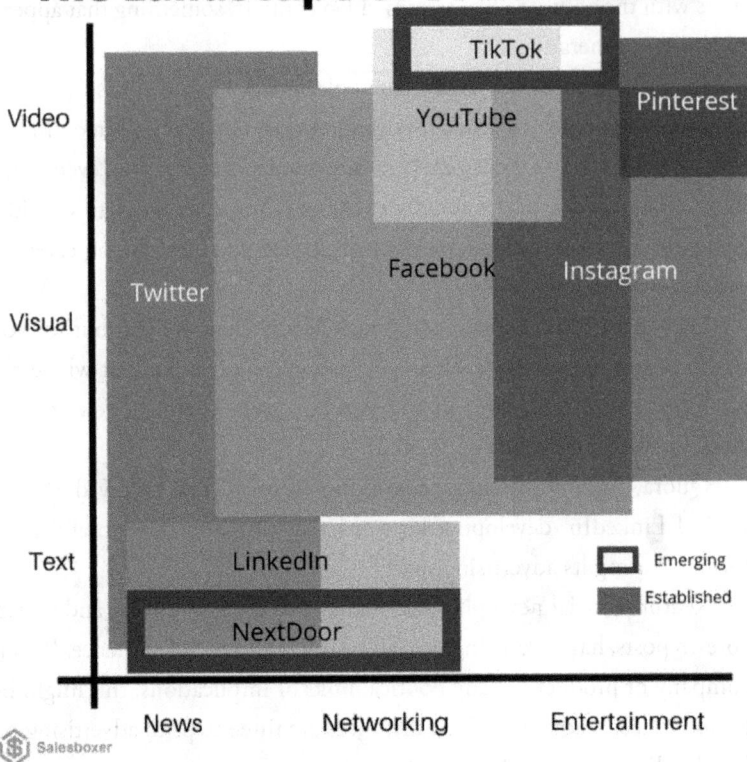

Figure 10.2 The landscape of social media

Developments in Advertising

Once you are familiar with the platforms and some of what they have to offer, you need to stay relevant by making sure you know what sort of advertising and audience-connecting options there are.

It can be overwhelming when faced with a world where the platforms and technology change continually, but once you join these social media sites, they will let you know when they have a new way to advertise or interact with your clientele. The onus will then be on you to make sure you learn how to use their new platforms.

Facebook, for example, is continuing to find new, creative, and dynamic ways to tailor ads to customers. They use machine learning, which can incorporate predictions about the type of customer base you will be able to reach, along with any information you input.

Currently, Facebook advertisers can tailor their ads to potential customers in several ways. First, you can give multiple text descriptions and let Facebook's algorithm determine what to show users, based on what the technology thinks the potential customer prefers. Secondly, there is an option to have ads automatically translated into whichever language your leads prefer, or you can provide translations.

Lastly, the ads can display many different formats and types of information about a product or service, which Facebook will determine based on what it seems the potential customer likes and responds to. Facebook currently offers this service for both paid and "organic" content.[8]

Facebook provides free courses to help its users learn more about social media advertising. These online courses cover using Facebook, Instagram, Messenger, or WhatsApp, and other linked social media.[9]

On other types of social media platforms, such as Quora, some advertising tools include behavior targeting, based on the customer's interests, keyword history, or question history. In contrast, you could use broad targeting instead, which is a general, maximized reach of advertising across a platform.

If you have a product or business that is best displayed visually, you might consider using Instagram ads.

There are several different kinds of ads to choose from on Instagram:

- Stories ads
- Photo ads
- Video ads
- Carousel ads
- Collection ads
- Ads in Explore

There are multiple formats you can try out or even alternate between, depending on what works for you. Some of the newer types of ads, including ads in Explore and Stories, offer unique options.

---

[8]Facebook. "Facebook for Business." facebook.com/business, (accessed January 1, 2020).

[9]Facebook. "Facebook Blueprint." facebook.com/business/learn, (accessed January 10, 2020).

Explore, for example, allows you to reach an audience that is craving new experiences. Consider these stats.

- *200 million*: Number of daily active accounts that turn to Instagram's Explore page
- *50 percent*: Percentage of accounts on Instagram that use Explore every month
- *83 percent*: Percentage of people surveyed who discover new products or services on Instagram

People want to investigate what's new and trendy. Explore allows your business to be part of that.

If you think you can't reach your audience through Instagram, another visual app that has been on the rise is Snapchat. Snapchat markets its ad space as being uniquely poised to reach an audience that doesn't necessarily spend time on Instagram and Facebook. They claim more than a third of their audience doesn't have a presence on either of those other platforms.[10]

Some reasons you may want to stay current by using Snapchat are:

- They reach a younger audience, with over 210 million users.
- Their ads are straightforward to use.
- You can tailor your ads to the category of your business. Experiment with snap ads, collection ads, stories ads, AR lenses, filters, or commercials.
- You can filter and choose your potential customer base by several advanced criteria, such as:
  - Interests and behavior
  - Demographics
  - Location
  - Look-alike audience

---

[10]Snap Inc. "Snapchat Ads for Every Business." forbusiness.snapchat.com, (accessed January 10, 2020).

If your business could benefit from video ads, YouTube might be worth exploring. YouTube has been a mega platform for a while now. It offers ads with multiple payment structures and the ability to expand or concentrate the reach of ads. Many small to medium-sized businesses have begun to advertise this way. Users of YouTube ads have the option to create and upload their original video content or to use providers that offer tools and services that can create professional video content.

With a wide age range regularly using YouTube throughout the day, businesses have the potential to reach many people. Their website is bursting with success stories of small businesses that made a small investment in YouTube advertising, which ended up growing their business tremendously. In addition, you get to choose who sees your ads to make them as effective as possible.[11]

As advertising on social media platforms develops, you need to learn how to use it. If this seems like an intimidating place to start, there is another route you can take that may prove just as effective.

Microinfluencers

In recent years, there has been a movement toward using microinfluencers on social media to promote a company or product. Instead of having to forge a relationship with a celebrity, companies now use those who have become influential in a specific space on social media.[12]

Influencers are ordinary people who have strategically gained a large following on various social media platforms. They have niche areas of interest, posting blogs, pictures, videos, or tweets gushing about how much they loved a product or service. Soon after, their followers rush to sign up.

A company called Sonnet James is one example of how an influencer can help a small business grow. The founder of the company, Whitney Lundeen, explained on a *Shark Tank* episode that her business grew overnight after a mommy blogger chose to feature her.

---

[11]YouTube. "YouTube Ads." youtube.com/ads, (accessed January 10, 2020).
[12]A. Corcione. 2019. "Future of Social Media: Trends to Watch." businessnewsdaily .com/10522-future-of-social-media-marketing.html, (accessed January 10, 2020).

Lundeen had created a versatile dress moms could both work and play in, to remind moms to play with their kids. She developed a website and e-mailed several influential bloggers to help spread the word.

One influential mommy blogger, Gabrielle Blair from Design Mom, liked the dress so much that she featured it on her blog. Over the next 2 days, orders poured in, without a way for Lundeen to fill them all. It forced her to expand, and her business took off from there.[13]

Lundeen's success story is only one example. There are microinfluencers in almost every niche today. They have become a natural part of spreading the word, as they already have a large following in the area of their interest.

Influencers are present across many different social media platforms, including YouTube, Instagram, and Snapchat. Influencers promote and present products in a positive light in several ways. They may order products and unbox them on video, examining them with excitement or interest.[14]

An example of this is in the toy industry. Both children and adults have become this type of influencer on YouTube. As many kids today watch YouTube, they are likely to stumble across these videos, making them want to buy the product.

One microinfluencer on YouTube, named Kelli Maple, has 1.26 million subscribers and gets many millions of views on her regular unboxing videos. She is only 16 years old but has been building a following for 5 years. She unboxes and plays with baby dolls and accessories, repeatedly mentioning the company she has received the product from.[15]

The microinfluencer market has grown continuously. Small businesses can and should jump on this bandwagon. Ultimately, it will drive traffic to your website, grow your customer base, and drive sales.

---

[13]BossLadies. "Whitney Lundeen of Sonnet James." bossladies.us/articles/sonnetjames, (accessed December 31, 2019).

[14]Digital Marketing Institute. "3 Trends Defining the Future of Social Media for Business." digitalmarketinginstitute.com/en-us/blog/3-trends-defining-the-future-of-social-media-for-business, (accessed January 10, 2020).

[15]"Kelli Maple." youtube.com/channel/UCFkW3zyiniJ9Dn8nLR8_v3w, (accessed December 31, 2020).

Visual Branding

Remember that the future of social media will always be in how you visually present your company. How do you recognize a brand? Look at the following images. How many could you match with the social media platforms we have been talking about (Figure 10.3)?

Figure 10.3 Some of the logos for current social media platforms

Hours of careful planning went into branding each of these platforms. The color, shapes, lines, text, and spacing each of these social media platforms chose to represent their brand were unique. They had to be, to be recognizable.

Additionally, these platforms have branded every place they advertise the same way. They are going to consistently use the same fonts, the same types of images, their logo, and the same color scheme. These tactics make it easy for users to recognize their brand immediately.

According to Ideas on Purpose, an NYC-based branding agency, "a logo or typographic brand mark—is your identity in its simplest form. It should immediately call to mind your organization—and (as importantly) call to heart the distinct emotional appeal at your brand's core."[16]

---

[16]Ideas on Purpose. "The 5 Essentials of Visual Branding," ideasonpurpose.com/on/the-5-essentials-of-visual-branding, (accessed January 17, 2020).

Developing a logo and spreading it across your social media is probably the most straightforward way to build brand recognition. But there is more to visual branding than having a logo.

You may want to start by asking yourself: What is going to be easily recognizable, yet unique, about the way you choose to visually represent your brand?

In choosing your visual branding, consider your options for the following elements:

1. Logo
2. Colors
3. Typography/fonts
4. Images
5. Spacing and style

Check out the following examples. Which ad is more engaging (Figure 10.4)?

Figure 10.4 Sylvie's Salon, take 1

In this first one, you might notice there are two different kinds of fonts divided by an unnecessary dark line. The image is abstract, with a woman's hair clearly displayed, but with no personality, as we cannot see her face (Figure 10.5).

Wake up like this EVERY DAY with Sylvie's Salon. #SylviesSalon
#BeBeautiful #NewHairDo

Book an appointment

Figure 10.5 Sylvie's Salon take 2

This second example represents a huge improvement to the ad. The designer has made the font consistent, making the salon name elegant, adding in a photo that focuses on hair, along with a much better message. The image is more tied to a local salon feel and uses a quirky message to attract attention.

Logo, images, text, and design all speak volumes about your brand, whether you realize it or not. Make sure not to forget these elements when looking forward to the future of social media.

Stories

One format that allows you to try out different styles of branding is Stories. The Story format isn't brand new, but it has started to gain traction on Instagram, Snapchat, Facebook, and YouTube. It has already played a vital role in social media marketing, and experts expect that to continue.

Stories within various social media platforms allow you to post a vibrant update that stays for 24 hours at the top of your audience's search feed. The update can include pictures and video meshed together.

One advantage to Stories is that they take up the entire screen of someone's phone once someone has clicked in, playing through photos, videos, stickers, text, and much more. The Stories feature on Snapchat and Instagram also offers face lenses, GIF integrations, and the ability to draw or write on material.[17] In a short time, you can share a story that will connect with your customers.[18]

If you're wondering if the bandwagon for Stories is only a passing fad, keep in mind:

- 96 percent of U.S. marketers plan to continue with Stories ads.
- One-third of the most viewed Instagram Stories are from businesses.
- 50 percent of businesses on Instagram worldwide are using Stories.[19]

Another advantage to using Stories is that they have ephemeral content that disappears after a day. This temporary nature allows companies to test-drive their content and view how well it engaged with customers.

You can use Stories to gain useful information, such as which days of the week attract the most attention, what type of content draws people, and much more. You don't have to worry about regretting content that flops, coloring others' overall impression of your account.

---

[17] Digital Marketing Institute. "3 Trends Defining the Future."

[18] Instagram. "Instagram Business." business.instagram.com/advertising, (accessed January 17, 2020).

[19] Instagram. "Instagram Stories." business.instagram.com/a/stories, (accessed January 17, 2020).

Just like images and videos, you can post stories across your social media channels. There are also options to make your Story interactive. To maximize the number of people who see your Story, you may want to tag those who are in it or would be interested in what it is about. Additionally, you can tag the location to draw a more local crowd.[20]

Some social media platforms have interactive options for Stories, such as swiping to take you to the product or company website. If you end up creating a story you are proud of, you can select the option for it to stay posted, instead of disappearing after the 24-hour period.[21]

Video Content

Along with Stories, video content has been and will continue to be vital to reaching an audience through social media.

Video content can do several things for potential and returning customers:

- Demonstrate a product or effectiveness of a service.[22]
- Build trust that a product is what it claims to be and works correctly.
- Engage customers by showing many possibilities of needing and interacting with a product, instead of being limited to a single image or collection of images.
- Make a customer feel more connected and "in the moment" with a product, company, or service.

Because of all these benefits, video has become an increasingly popular format for connecting companies with potential clientele. Many marketing professionals have claimed video content has the best return on investment (ROI).[23]

---

[20]A. Bowman. "Why Social Media Stories Are a Big Marketing Phenomenon." advertisingweek360.com/why-social-media-stories-are-a-big-marketing-phenomenon, (Accessed January 17, 2020).

[21]Ibid.

[22]Digital Marketing Institute. "3 Trends Defining the Future."

[23]Ibid.

With video and visual content on the rise, it's essential to get the aesthetic and design aspects as close to perfect as possible for your business.

Augmented Reality

Along with video content, advances in augmented reality are important to think about for the future, as these will most likely play an important role in social media marketing. Basically, augmented reality allows a customer to try something on for size in the digital world.[24]

Facebook has been a pioneer of this strategy, using options for a customer to "digitally sample makeup and accessories, allowing them to model how they look with them before buying anything."[25] Look for emerging social media platforms that are based on augmented reality for users.

Content Remains King

The key to the future of social media is keeping customers engaged through relevant, engaging content. Content has always been, and will remain, king for a brand and a company. But with the future of technology and social media, the content may change forms.

Remember, the customer has an overflow of information in their news feed. If they don't see something that immediately grabs their interest, you will lose an opportunity to connect.

Where do you start? What is the best way to get customers to engage with your posts in the uncharted territory of social media and its future? In many ways, you can draw inspiration from the areas to move forward based on principles of the past and present.

---

[24]G. Constantin. "What Is the Future of Social Media Marketing?" thriveglobal.com/stories/what-is-the-future-of-social-media-marketing, (accessed December 31, 2019).
[25]Expert commentator. 2019. "5 Ways to Use Augmented Reality in Your Marketing Strategy." smartinsights.com/digital-marketing-platforms/augmented-reality/5-ways-to-use-augmented-reality-in-your-marketing-strategy, (accessed January 20, 2020).

1. Publish Relevant Content

Start with being relevant.[26] Get in touch with your followers in how they live their lives. Ask questions. Poll them. Figure out what connects with them and post about it. It could be anything from a funny meme to a beautiful photo or a relatable anecdote.

2. Educate

Next, ask yourself how you are educating your customers through what you post.[27] Are you sharing interesting, relevant statistics? Do you have video content of people using your product or service so people can see for themselves how to use it?

You need to let your customers know not only that you are an authority in your area of business, but also that you can teach them about it.[28]

3. Be Authentic

Share about the behind-the-scenes vision and mission of your company. Be transparent. Customers will flock to your authenticity.[29]

For example, which of the following seems more genuine and would draw your trust and loyalty as a potential client (Figure 10.6)?

If you saw this ad on Facebook, you might be skeptical. Is there an IT support and repair company that would confidently claim they can solve *every* problem? Your experience may tell you otherwise, and you would therefore move on, assuming the company is making a promise they cannot deliver on.

---

[26]L. Marcyes. "7 Smart Strategies to Take Your Social Media to the Next Level." blogs. oracle.com/marketingcloud/seven-smart-strategies-to-take-your-social-media-to-the-next-level, (accessed January 9, 2020).

[27]Ibid.

[28]V. Schmid. "Why Social Media Is Important for Business Marketing." marketinginsidergroup.com/content-marketing/why-social-media-is-important-for-business-marketing, (accessed November 15, 2019).

[29]Ibid.

F. I. X. I. T

We can solve every technology problem.

Figure 10.6 F.I.X.I.T., take 1

However, if the ad you saw looked more like this (Figure 10.7):

Don't pull your hair out...let us solve your tech issues.
#TechHelp #FIXIT #YourTechProblemsSolved

F. I. X. I. T
24/7 Tech Help

Message Us

Figure 10.7 F.I.X.I.T., take 2

You might pause to investigate. Offering tech support around the clock is a valuable service, and with connections around the world, this has become more possible. The message "Avoid premature wrinkles..." caters to those who are younger and in need of tech support. In this type of ad, the message and picture could be changed to target different demographics to reach even more customers.

Being authentic doesn't mean you need to flaunt your limitations or flaws. It does mean, however, that you need to show that you understand and respect your audience. Remember to listen to feedback and track what people are saying about your company on social media. How can you address their concerns? How can you capitalize on their praise?

Do your homework on other brands that are similar to yours, and insert yourself into relevant conversations concerning that brand or your area.

Incorporate interesting ideas where you see others finding success, as this can help you navigate the future of social media. But along the way, don't innovate yourself away from the true heart and voice of your brand. Figure out how to synthesize trends with what your company has to offer and say. If a specific trend can't fit with your brand, move on. There will be plenty more trends to join along the way.[30]

4. Be Unique

Don't underestimate the importance of making your content unique.[31] Does it stand out? If not, you could find yourself tuned out. Customers will see your posts and continue on their way, lumping you along with other companies that are posting the same type of posts you are.

What is the quality of your posts?[32] Are you checking your spelling and grammar? If you have video content or pictures, you need them to be appealing and of high quality. Customers won't watch your videos if the sound keeps cutting out, and they won't give a blurry, dark photo a second look.

---

[30]Corcione. "Future of Social Media: Trends to Watch."
[31]Marcyes. "7 Smart Strategies."
[32]Ibid.

Make the type of posts fit your brand. Your brand will determine the platforms you use, the types of media you use, and the overall feel of your posts.[33] If you are trying to give off a professional, credible vibe within the medical space, don't post videos of kittens playing. If you are a light-hearted, personable company, you will want to embrace that by posting pictures, videos, stories, and memes to showcase that.

One of the primary reasons social media has the potential to be your most effective marketing platform is that it provides instant feedback. Even if a post gets no likes and no comments, the lack of engagement is feedback in itself. The content was most likely not interesting or didn't connect with anyone.

One of the best things about social media is that you can try out many kinds of posts. When you are using free marketing through social media, you have some wiggle room to find your groove. If at first you don't succeed, you can try, try, try again!

If you are paying for your social media marketing by the advertisement or boost, you may want to be more conservative in what you try. That makes it even more vital to get to know your audience on the front end. Ask open-ended questions to solicit opinions! Try out a free post or two to see what grabs your audience's attention before you pay for one.

5. Start Small

Lastly, when creating content, start small. Try to do it well before you spread yourself too thin. Choose one or two types of content you want to get good at, and focus on those.

Select one platform to be your main marketing avenue, and invest in getting to know how it works. Experiment to see what you can sustain and afford and what seems to get the best response before you branch out.

You don't want to end up managing ad campaigns on multiple platforms before you realize you would have been better off going in another direction.

---

[33]D. Hall. 2017. "4 Easy Ways to Take Social Media Marketing to the Next Level." marketingland.com/4-easy-ways-take-social-media-marketing-next-level-223025, (accessed November 10, 2019).

Remember that through all the changes and evolutions of social media, content will always be king as you represent your brand. Be authentic and engaging with your product or service, and you will be able to successfully reach and interact with your audience through social media.

Chapter 10: Key Takeaways

After reading this chapter, what should you understand?

1. It's smart to stay on top of emerging social platforms, in addition to maintaining an active presence on established ones such as Facebook and LinkedIn.
2. You can stay relevant by familiarizing yourself with the advertising options on newer platforms such as Snapchat, which can help you expand your reach to a different audience.
3. Remember the landscape of social media, and be strategic about which platforms will do the best for your business.
4. Find microinfluencers within your niche or industry, and reach out to explore a partnership.
5. Use your logo when posting visual content.
6. With authentic, relevant, valuable, and interesting content, you will continue to grow your audience across all social platforms you choose to use for your online marketing.

CHAPTER 11

Hear from Those Who Have Done It Well

At this point, you have heard all the theory and practical steps to take. Now, let's examine some real-world examples of people who have successfully used social media to expand their clientele and grow their businesses.

These are businesses that started out just like yours, adding one customer and sale at a time. They have already tested the waters on various social media platforms, and the insights they have to offer are invaluable.

Here is a little taste of the small businesses we connected with to learn about their success using social media.

- *College Hunks* is a quick-growing business that started locally in Washington, DC, and has expanded to many areas of the United States. They focus on providing quality service in the area of packing, unpacking, moving, and removing items for homes and businesses. We want to show you how they have shared their brand and their value of building leaders in their company with clientele in a way that is approachable and fresh.
- *The Catch Company* provides the latest and greatest gear for fishing fanatics. They use social media to display their products while sharing some lighthearted humor with fellow fishers.
- *EncoreGarage*, a nationwide, full-service garage improvement company, provides epoxy floor coatings, cabinetry, garage organization systems, and more. They rely on Instagram to post photos and videos of their work and on Facebook to run ads promoting their business.
- *Tripton Real Estate*, based in Winnetka and servicing the Chicago area, has done a wonderful job of creating a visually appealing Instagram page. They paint a picture of luxurious properties and

successful home sales, which will appeal to anyone looking to buy or sell.

- *Winestyr*, a wine distribution company, is passionate about finding and sharing great wines, while supporting small business owners. They have gathered a large following on Instagram for good reason. They are fantastic storytellers in a visually appealing and sensory-oriented way.

It doesn't take an expert to figure out how to create a business profile on Facebook or to set up an Instagram account. Any business owner with the desire to develop a following on social media can do so, following in the footsteps of these other small businesses.

As you read these stories, you may want to reflect on how you use social media for your business. *Is your business like any of these? Is there a way you can be more visually appealing, tell your story better, or learn how to network further?*

Case Studies

Sarah Vaile Design

Sarah Vaile got her start in design in New York, founded her company in 2008, and quickly gained a fantastic reputation. Her Instagram page, paired with her visually stunning and well-designed website, focuses on images of beautiful interior and architectural designs, as well as other publications that have featured her company's work.

Vaile also uses social media to showcase her work in progress, new staff she has hired, and excitement about finishing a project. In short, Sarah Vaile Design strikes just the right balance in showing visually stunning photos with being authentic. They have found that the posts that engage people the most are visually stunning kitchens and bathrooms, especially if they feature blue.

On the Sarah Vaile Design website, she also has a blog, where she shares the stories of her process. She draws in potential customers through easy-to-read instructions and tips and tricks to create great designs.

Sarah Vaile Design didn't gain their 9,900+ followers on Instagram overnight. They have learned to post regularly and have connected with influencers and popular sites that feature their work. They have watched many other businesses' followers start following them after being featured on their page.

Vaile has found it to be "a symbiotic relationship with the shelter magazines, lines of the trade, bloggers and other designers." Getting connected with others in her space has been a powerful tool in getting her name out there.

Vaile's employees have loved sharing about their ongoing projects on their Instagram and social media accounts, which Vaile encourages and has found helpful in growing their influence.

Vaile foresees social media marketing as taking the place of traditional advertising. She sees influencers as being a prominent part of this. She thinks it will become essential and ever more important to stay transparent and genuine. When people think something looks too good, it only adds to someone's "inferiority complex where everyone's else life appears richer, happier, more perfect."

Lou Malnati's Pizzeria

Lou Malnati's has earned a reputation in the Chicago and Phoenix areas for great pizza, aided in part by their posts on social media. According to Beth Gerage, the marketing communications content developer, social media functions as "a recruiting tool," "a selling platform," and sometimes a "customer service tool."

Gerage's favorite social media site is Instagram. They use it to show "delicious-looking pictures of our pizza with our fans," as well as to spread the word about contests, promotions, and giveaways. Their photos are genuine, showing people they have collaborated with influencers on social media "to reach new audiences and grow awareness" for their brand.

The types of posts Gerage has found engage people the most are cheesy pizza photos and funny memes and videos. Gerage and her team take trending memes and make it relevant to their brand. When a meme featuring Baby Yoda holding a teacup became popular, for example, they used it to promote their brand by changing it to a coffee cup with Lou Malnati's written on it, captioning it with: "When your friends are fighting over which deep dish to order... #LousForLife."

Lou Malnati's take advantage of social media to create video content, sharing about menu items, connecting with the holidays, or promoting any special events. For example, for Halloween, they showed a video of costumed children coming to Lou Malnati's to trick-or-treat and happily receiving free pieces of pizza. The tone of the video was warm and neighborly, as if Lou Malnati's was saying, "We want to be part of your community." It fitted perfectly with their local pizza place brand.

The holiday postings for Lou Malnati's are the product of careful planning. They mark any special holidays and other days of the year that are important to their business. Then, Gerage and her team will create and schedule their posts at least a week in advance. That way, if anything comes up, they have some flexibility.

Impressively, Lou Malnati's has gained over 54,900 followers and is still growing. The key to gaining a large following on Instagram? They started posting almost daily, using influencers to help them spread the word.

Employees can sometimes contribute to social media as well, whether through reposting photos or funny memes to their stories on their social media accounts or sharing a recruiting post.

Recently, Lou Malnati's has begun to experiment with social media advertising, exploring tools that will help them track their impact on all social media platforms. Gerage and her team intend to stay up to date on trends in social media to continue growing their customer base.

Abby Dunn PR and Consulting

With over 15 years of experience in consulting and handling public relations for well-known clients, Abby Dunn has done her homework on using social media effectively.

She uses it regularly to create a buzz around a company, person, or product. She knows that effective use of social media can translate directly into sales, making it a crucial asset to marketing.

Dunn has found Instagram to be a powerful tool to create a powerful visual impact for her clients. She works hard to make the posts communicate authenticity, as those are the kinds of posts that draw the most attention. She makes sure companies establish clear goals, which form an overall strategy for promoting their business on social media. She then helps them achieve those goals step by step.

Dunn has encouraged clients to take advantage of the attention and following they can gain through Instagram. One example of this is Gibson's Steakhouse, whose Instagram page shows bright, attractive photos of the food and restaurant. She stages some of the photos, but takes many in the moment, with customers and employees. Dunn might also take fun, behind-the-scenes photos of the restaurant getting ready to open for a celebration.

Dunn has found hashtags effective in drawing like-minded individuals to their page. For Gibson's Steakhouse, this meant using many Chicago and food-themed hashtags. Around the holidays, they throw in some holiday-themed hashtags as well.

Dunn anticipates each new generation will latch on to their version of social media, meaning that companies will need to continually adapt if they want to continue to reach the current generation. She has found Facebook has become more and more "for old people" in the eyes of Gen Z, who choose to use Snapchat and TikTok instead.

Winestyr

Winestyr is an online wine club that provides people with access to wines and wineries that they otherwise wouldn't be able to access. Winestyr has an elegant Instagram page full of gorgeous vineyard landscape shots, sophisticated photos of wine bottles, photos portraying various stages of winemaking, endearing photos of the winemakers, and shots of employees who taste and select the wines. They have even added video content with a vlog of the new wines they find to showcase to their customers.

Winestyr makes generous and effective use of hashtags, bringing lots of traffic that has helped them gain nearly 14,000 followers and get likes and comments on every post.

As Erin Althoff, vice president of business development, cited the following reasons for why they feel social media is so important to their business:

> You can curate content and messaging to educate, inform, and inspire—all from your company's unique voice. You also have the opportunity to not just talk at your audience, like some traditional marketing channels, but really engage in conversations and make lasting impressions.

Winestyr has found that the posts that engage people the most are experiential ones showing ways and places people can enjoy their wines.

On Facebook, Winestyr has a growing presence as well. They found this platform gained even more traction when they opened a showroom in Chicago. They allow guests to check in at their location, bringing a broader awareness of their company.

Gifted for You

Brenna Nichols, owner and founder of Gifted For You, has found social media to be an essential marketing and advertising platform for her business. As Nichols has a limited budget for the advertising costs, Instagram has served as a means for her to reach a wide clientele.

Nichols has over 1,400 followers already, and with her regular, colorful and appealing posts, she is sure to gain many more. Nichols has gained all of her followers organically, explaining that "having authentic followers (vs. paid followers) is better for my business because it's the authentic followers who will actually hire me."

Nichols has also been able to connect with other companies and business partners through Instagram. She follows 2,230 people and businesses, exemplifying the principle that to get followers, you need to actively follow others.

Nichols has found that telling the story of how each gift her company has provided came to be is a visually impactful way to draw people in. Nichols has had many clients share the gifts they have given or received on social media. These posts help organically spread the word about her company and her many satisfied customers.

Amigos Restaurants

Amigos Restaurants is a fresh, quick service restaurant chain in the Midwest that delights in pleasing their customers. Jan Moore, founder and VP of marketing for Amigos Restaurants, loves to use social media to spread awareness of their brand, mainly because it has a growing audience and can continually target a new, younger following.

Currently, the largest social media presence for Amigos is on Facebook, but they use Twitter and Instagram as well. They link their Twitter and Instagram posts to their Facebook page, getting potentially twice as many, if not more, views per post. Their Facebook has over 8,660 followers, their Twitter has 1,200+ followers, and their Instagram has 961 followers.

Moore and her team have purposefully used Facebook as their main platform, wanting to target an older crowd of moms and people over 35 years old.

The posts that have generated the most interaction for Amigos ask the viewer to do something. For example, Amigos often promises small gift cards to a random drawing to people who respond to their posts, which ask questions such as "What's your favorite winter weather activity?"

Moore and her team also like to feature unique items such as their "Yankee" burrito or advertise for free delivery for celebrations such as the Super Bowl. Their posts almost always include a picture of their food and may include a satisfied customer enjoying it.

Moore and her team try to make all their photos as appealing as possible by using filters and editing to highlight the pleasant aspects of the food. They are strategic in posting their Kopeli Coffee pictures early in the morning and their food specials around 10 or 10:30 a.m., when people will start getting hungry for lunch. They have a contest for a small gift card every Friday around the same time, so their customers have some predictability. They wait to pick a winner until Monday so that they can be sure people will be engaging with their Friday post over the weekend.

Moore and her team have found it effective to promote their social media posts by putting a little money behind them. In addition, once they added the element of the weekly contests, they saw their following increasing. They have followed the simple recipe of staying true to their homestyle Mexican brand while posting frequently and relevantly.

Another fun and successful strategy that Amigos uses on social media is sharing about former employees and where they are now. These posts get in front of new audiences, which bring in new followers (and potential customers!) they wouldn't otherwise reach. Additionally, Moore and her team like to share posts about coworkers who receive positive feedback from customers, which gets shared with their friends and family.

Lisa Kinzelberg Art

As the artist and owner behind the eponymous Lisa Kinzelberg Art, Kinzelberg got her start online through Instagram. Instagram was the perfect place to post her visual product to connect with existing contacts and make some new connections. She has found Instagram to be a good way to connect with people who enjoy creative works and the artistic process. She has been able to connect with people who are interested in art, fashion, home, lifestyle, and travel. She now has 468 followers and is continuing to grow.

Kinzelberg uses her Instagram account to keep her followers up to date. She shares pictures of herself working on projects, with friends and clients, and of her art being featured in various locations.

Kinzelberg especially loves Instagram's filters, which can translate the real-life beauty of her artwork to people's screens. Beautiful photos get some interaction and feedback, but Kinzelberg has discovered that people are more engaged when she is in the picture with her artwork, giving people a look at the artist behind it. Additionally, she gets more likes and comments when she shares any media coverage or upcoming art show information.

Her Instagram account began to gain traction around the time of her first art show. She also started following many other people on Instagram, and they returned the favor by following her back.

In the future, Kinzelberg hopes to stay relevant by using video and stories features on social media, as these tend to be more engaging. She wants to give the more personal, close-up feel that stories and videos offer, so that people will continue to connect with her and her brand. In addition to Instagram, Kinzelberg also uses LinkedIn.

Now that Kinzelberg has created a website, she can feature her artwork for sale on it. People can easily access more information about her, as well as see photos of projects she completed for clients.

Company + Cottage

Company + Cottage's website lends a charming, vacation-like, homey farmhouse feel. What started as a personal project of restoring a broken-down cottage for their family turned into a passion.

Christine Bridger and her husband offer the following description on their elegantly designed website:

> Over the past eight years, we have restored decrepit cottages that no one wanted, helped local businesses thrive and increased tourism through national press. What started out as a way to create beautiful spaces and memories for our family has turned into an opportunity for us to open our doors to others.

Customers who visit their website can rent or purchase their specially "handcrafted and curated cottages."

Their website and Instagram page, which has over 10,600 followers, picture founder Christine Bridger and her family enjoying the beautiful cottage they created together. There are photos of them enjoying spending time with one another, at work and play. The photos send a message that Company + Cottage is family oriented. They exemplify the type of lifestyle that they invite others to emulate.

There are countless photos of beautiful properties Bridger has designed and restored. Additionally, she shares steps she had to take along the way, like passing a real estate exam.

The posts Bridger has found that engage people the most are ones that are aspirational, such as "renovating a 1906 barn, board by board," or giving access to authentic, real-life moments. She likes to share pieces of stories over time, like updates on progress or setbacks in her personal and professional life.

She notes the struggle to post authentic content sometimes, nicknaming the phenomenon "post paralysis." She fears that certain posts will not match her previous level of content and will somehow taint her social media following and pages.

Regardless, she presses on, posting once or twice a week. She says she has found mornings to be the sweet spot for getting the most engagement.

Her success in social media has come from forming a clear, engaging brand, consistent voice and message, and national press. Each of these contributed to getting the word out and drawing in more potential customers.

NEAT Method

NEAT Method is all about organizing and designing a functional space for their clients' lifestyles. From their elegant webpage design to the well-done, interesting and informative video on their website, the ladies behind this business send an authentic message about their brand: They can make your life brighter, tidier, and more beautiful.

The tone they set is professional, yet personal, sharing about their journey in building their business together. They stay true to communicating their passion for organization on each platform, with memorable, authentic images and hashtags.

With over 585,000 followers on Instagram and thousands of likes on every post, you might say they've mastered this social media platform. They post visually appealing, bright photos of beautifully organized spaces and projects they've completed. Additionally, they use Instagram to post job openings.

Their posts aren't just beautiful; they're also informative. They display new ways of thinking about maximizing space and making areas neat and organized. It's no wonder these are the posts that get the most engagement.

Though their original motivation for using social media was as a marketing tool, they have also found it useful to connect with and educate their followers about organization.

They have created events centered on organizing, such as their #newyearNEATme challenge, which challenges their followers to organize one space of their lives each day. These posts have connected with the needs of their audience and garnered much engagement.

Success on social media didn't happen overnight for them. They have steadily posted once a day, finding the time each day that works the best. They have discovered that the key to gaining a large, steady following on Instagram turned out to be hiring an employee to focus on spreading the word about their brand on social media. She was able to devote the time to engage with followers, run analytics, and curate content.

As Marissa Hagmeyer, CEO of Neat Method, shared, their motto on social media has always been quality over quantity, and they intend to keep it that way. They will continue to make sure each post is well designed and thoughtfully created, ensuring that they maintain the interest and excitement around their business.

Tripton Real Estate

As a Realtor, Bonnie Tripton knows the power of referrals. She uses social media posts to help get the word out about her business and success.

She has relied mainly on Facebook and Instagram. She has gathered 106 followers on Facebook, who comment on and like some of her posts. On Instagram, she has a growing group of 414 followers.

Tripton Instagram account consists of pictures of her success stories. Anyone happening upon her page would see that she regularly and successfully sells beautiful properties in Chicago's north side and in the city. People like and engage with her posts with pictures of "homes that look like they are out of a magazine."

She has also bought some Instagram ads and connected with interior designers on Instagram. Both strategies have helped bolster her traffic and response.

Her regular posts on Instagram keep her top of mind among her satisfied customers. Some of the customers who see her posts have referred her to friends who are looking for a property.

Tripton feels social media is "a way to target your sphere and keep them in the loop on your business." And the best part is, it's affordable advertising.

Shri Yoga

Marcia Tazioli, the owner of Shri Yoga, uses social media to effectively market her business. One of her most successful social media campaigns was when she began posting teasers that "something new" was coming to her yoga studio. By keeping it a mystery, she noticed that the yoga community responded with excitement and interest. When she finally revealed that it was a new inferno hot Pilates class, she made a big deal out of it, and people responded on social media. She also offered some free classes as part of a promotion and found that generating excitement around those on social media brought a lot of people to them. Many who attended the free classes signed up for her Pilates classes.

Since day one of the 8 years Shri Yoga has been in business, Tazioli has been promoting it on social media. Though she started by focusing on Facebook, she has found Instagram to be more effective, especially as she can share her Instagram posts on her Facebook page, thereby not losing any of her Facebook followers by focusing on Instagram.

Tazioli has found it effective to tag people's names, locations, and relevant terms to maximize the number of people who see her posts. She also recommends spending a little money to boost posts on occasion, as she recently boosted a post for $100 and noticed 3,000 people saw it.

She has found that simple, beautiful, and inspirational posts get the most attention. Some examples of such posts are photos of instructors doing poses in the studio. She uses these posts to share about the benefits of the pose and to list a schedule for classes. She always tags the teacher's name and creates as many hashtags of the pose and the teacher as possible.

Additionally, she tries to educate and inspire others through her posts, whether it is a class schedule, an inspirational quote, a health tip, or about a new teacher or class. She will also post group photos of students in her classes and tag the students' names. That way, more people see the post, share it, and like it. Tazioli also saw a large response from people to a photo she shared of her 6-year-old son at the yoga studio, as people thought it was cute.

Tazioli also uses social media to stay relevant, posting about holidays and responding to a death or a natural disaster. She takes every opportunity to honor her community and show her compassion. She has been able to use social media to define her business as a positive, upbeat yoga studio that cares about people and inspires them.

Social media has enabled Tazioli to build her brand, recruit new students, promote her teachers, show off the beautiful space, share information about what kind of classes they teach, and to drive new business to the space for classes, teacher training, and workshops. Her Facebook following has grown to nearly 1,500, and her Instagram page has over 1,000 followers. People have begun to hear about her yoga studio and come from surrounding areas for classes and teacher training.

She couldn't have done it alone, either. Her teachers all share posts of their classes on Facebook and Instagram, checking in at her studio and using hashtags to promote it. She has found that the teachers who post on social media get more people attending their classes.

Tazioli thinks that the more social media tools she can use, the better, and hopes to expand to include Snapchat, Twitter, and LinkedIn as regular tools in her promotional efforts in the future.

KBK Communications

KBK Communications is a digital marketing agency focused on the health care industry. Nicole Tullis, director of social media management at KBK Communications, knows the importance of using social media for marketing. Their company helps health care-related companies market themselves on all platforms, including social media.

From the health care feel and design on their website to their LinkedIn profile, which boasts over 200 followers, to their Twitter, where their over 4,000 followers see their almost daily tweets, it's clear that KBK Communications is professional, sleek, and in the loop with the health care world.

KBK Communications has successfully used its social media platforms to create relationships with their clients and followers, to spread awareness of their brand, and to provide a continuous stream of educational information and resources.

KBK Communications has found that, because of the specific niche they are in, they are best able to connect with others on LinkedIn. Their audience on LinkedIn has been "more willing to engage with company updates, product releases, and stories on how products/services have impacted and influenced other companies."

On Facebook, they have discovered that showing a more emotional, relatable side of their company is crucial to getting more engagement. Personal content, such as images of customers using products, are usually the types of posts that foster engagement across the platforms. Tullis has gotten the sense that their audience is more willing to engage with their posts and their brand if it comes across as real, genuine, and relatable.

Tullis and her team have also noticed people will engage more if what they are posting is relevant content on social media such as a meme, a trending hashtag, or a popular video. When posting such timely updates, Tullis and her team show the connection their company has to it to send the message that they are still being true to their brand. The types of posts that don't get much engagement are those with selling content. People don't want to engage with an advertisement as much as with something they feel is authentic.

To gain their followers, Tullis has found it effective to use paid ads and organic content. They have to test and retest types of posts to see what works, as the social media world is always changing. They have noticed that what worked for them yesterday won't necessarily work for them today. As Tullis says, "Optimization is the key to marketing success."

KBK encourages their clients to get their employees involved in social media marketing. They do this through creating contests to see which employee shares the most content or generating excitement around posting what the company is doing on social media. KBK does this themselves as well, occasionally featuring a KBK employee on Facebook.

KBK tries to stay abreast of their industry, posting news that is relevant to their area as soon as they can. For their clients, they meticulously plan each day of posts for the coming month so they have time to create and curate effective posts.

Tullis thinks business websites may become unnecessary in the future, as many clients and customers primarily find companies and products through Facebook. This will save money for businesses as well. She thinks it is essential for businesses to learn how to use social media, and KBK has created an 8-week digital marketing strategy certification course. This course can help companies better align their marketing goals with successful strategies and techniques.

Bay Equity Home Loans

Three brothers and their friends started Bay Equity Home Loans in 2007. They brand themselves as a family that values helping their clients make their house a home.

The company has grown from a small home loans business into one of the top 30 home mortgage companies in the country.[1]

Their business relies heavily on technology, making the application process easy and efficient. However, that doesn't mean it has to be impersonal. From the warm, inviting, homey design of their website to their seasonally appropriate Facebook posts, potential customers can see the company cares enough to connect with them and their experience.

The company mostly uses their social media to spread the word about their brand. They reach a wide customer base through Facebook, posting many well-designed graphics and videos that show their personalized, service-oriented approach.

They have numerous Facebook pages, one for each region of the country. This approach allows the finance officer who oversees each area to connect with the population. It also means their posts can connect more specifically with the interests and culture of that area.

Janice Lake, a co-owner of Bay Equity Home Loans, mentioned that their employees post about the nonprofit organizations they support. They try to show who they are as people on social media so their customers view them as friends.

The Catch Company

The Catch Company is an aptly named fishing gear provider that started as a small business. They have grown into a successful and trusted brand, building on their principles of creating quality products and a fun experience for fishing fans.

The Catch Company strives to use social media to build a personal connection with their customers. Instead of relying on expensive advertising, they use social media to tell stories that will captivate and connect with their audience.

Ross Gordon, the company's CEO, is a personal fan of Instagram for the business as this platform can show rather than tell their audience the excellence of their product and brand. He also feels it reaches a broader audience than other social media avenues.

---

[1] *bayequityhomeloans.com/about-us*. Accessed December 5, 2019.

He employs humor in his posts, such as goofy pictures of employees or customers holding and using his products. His "chief fishing officer" stands in as a funny character of sorts, being featured in many of the photos and posts.

To demonstrate how well the product works, there are numerous photos of staff from the company, as well as customers, holding up their impressive catches.

On Facebook, Catch Company has amassed over 700,000 followers. They have had consistent growth over the years, linking it with their Instagram posts and video content.

Gordon has had success in connecting with others on LinkedIn as well. He uses it to share his professional knowledge and connect with like-minded businesspeople. He posts updates on how his business has been progressing, which potential investors or partners can see. Many have already connected with him through LinkedIn.

Over the years, Gordon's success in using social media has been a pivotal contributor to growing and keeping his clientele.

College Hunks Hauling Junk

What started in 2004 as two college guys who wanted to make a business out of packing, unpacking, and—well—hauling junk became a nationwide success. It didn't happen overnight. They started as a local company that used social media to help boost their business.

"Using social media for our business is necessary to stay relevant in the world we live in," said Nick Friedman, cofounder and president of College Hunks. They recognized it was an essential component to building a successful business early on.

College Hunks makes sure their posts on social media, such as Facebook, show what their brand is all about. Their posts consist of funny videos about moving, sentimental photos of those they have helped move, stories in video format, and an effective use of hashtags. All of these represent their values, which include "listen[ing], fulfill[ing] and delight[ing]; building leaders; [building a] fun, enthusiastic team environment."

Building leaders is one of the things people admire most about College Hunks, according to the feedback they have gotten from people liking those types of posts on social media. They share stories of what their previous employees have gone on to do, such as "become professional athletes, business owners, and parents." People love the inspiring and personal connection to the company, which means more followers and potentially more customers.

On Instagram, College Hunks posts plenty of lighthearted and playful pictures. They make good use of hashtags, adding ones that might attract an audience who wouldn't have otherwise come across them.

With over 18,000 followers on Facebook, College Hunks continues to reach a large client base, with potential to reach more, through the posts employees upload.

They place a high value on social media and its ability to get their name out. As Friedman put it, "Social media is literally only a click away from reaching and impacting a future client or engaging with existing client or employee."

Overall, social media has contributed to a growing awareness of the College Hunks company, which means when people who are now connected with the business need something moved or hauled away, they will automatically think of College Hunks.

EncoreGarage

Tony Scaletta's garage enhancement business, EncoreGarage, provides services in garage improvements and enhancements, including floor coatings, storage, organization, and cabinetry. EncoreGarage has successfully used social media to create brand awareness and generate leads. Scaletta has found Instagram and Facebook to be the most helpful in accomplishing his marketing goals.

On Instagram, Scaletta has gathered over 1,100 followers. He regularly posts examples of the work being done at EncoreGarage, including before-and-after photos his employees have taken, so viewers can see the amazing results. He has found Instagram to be an easy platform for him to visually demonstrate his company's work and to gain followers.

Video has proven to be an effective tool, showing their process as they work. Eye-catching videos such as blending metallic epoxies over a floor have been the most popular. He tries to post once a day, linking his Instagram with his Facebook page.

Scaletta likes using Facebook's tools for running ads and has been able to catch the interest of 380 followers. He hopes to spend more money to run ads, as he feels Facebook is the best way to reach potential customers.

In addition, Scaletta has a LinkedIn page, which he has used to connect with more than 450 others. He posts informative articles about how to work on various areas of a garage. He also shares some of his Instagram posts to his LinkedIn.

In the future, Scaletta thinks social media will become increasingly competitive and expensive. For now, he realizes the importance for businesses to have a strong presence on social media to be competitive. He intends to continue to improve his post content in an effort to attract more clientele.

Chapter 11: Key Takeaways

After reading this chapter, what should you understand?

1. Any business can learn how to harness the power of social media to grow their reach and their brand.
2. Many different companies have found success in sharing funny, relatable posts featuring photos of their staff or customers interacting with their products.
3. Posting regularly on your chosen platform(s) keeps you top of mind among your followers and encourages them to be part of the conversation.
4. Have a consistent voice and message to grow your audience organically.
5. Experiment with different types of content on various platforms to learn what "sticks" with your followers.

APPENDIX

Sample Social Media Plans

Figure A1

Salesboxer's Plan for Indoor Water Conservation

Customized Social Media and Facebook Advertising Plan

- Post to Facebook
- Post to Twitter
- Post to LinkedIn
- Post to Instagram
- Manage YouTube to increase engagement
- Facebook advertising targeted toward page
- Create customized hashtags to further brand your social media platforms
- Monitor software to understand peak engagement times for your platforms
- Customer review graphics and/or graphics made with photos of your work

Customized E-mails

- Manage your e-mail addresses within your system
- Send e-mails to your list of contacts

Hashtag Ideas

Customized Hashtags
#IndoorWaterConservation
#IndoorH2O
#WaterCostsReduced
#WaterFlowLimiter
#WaterEfficiencyPartner

Market Hashtags
#HotelWaterEfficiency
#MultiFamilyWaterEfficiency

Searched Hashtags
#WaterEfficiency
#WaterUseEfficiency

Primary Goal for Indoor Water Conservation on Social Media

Generate brand name recognition for Indoor Water Conservation for their B-to-B clients like hotel owners and multifamily unit owners.

Website:

https://indoorwaterconservation.com

Editorial Calendar for Posts

* Focus on special social media days and video releases
Q1: New Year's
Q2: Earth Day, Summer Preparation, Mother's Day, Memorial Day, Father's Day
Q3: Fourth of July
Q4: Halloween, Holidays

DIRECT 🎵 CARPET ONE FLOOR & HOME

Direct Carpet One
Social Media Marketing Plan

Platforms	Key Events
Facebook Twitter Instagram	Store giveaways Store openings
Primary Goal	**What Makes Us Special**
Generate recognition for Direct Carpet One and store opening in Goodyear, AZ	Customers are online and like to see fresh, modern design and difference of our product
Customized Hashtags	**Searched Hashtags**
#PickDirectCarpetOne #DirectCarpetOne #DoDirectCarpetOne	#carpetinstallation #beautifulcarpet #hardwoodflooring

$ Salesboxer

Figure A2

Salesboxer
Content Development Worksheet
Mentor Agility

Date: _____

Target: *What is the primary target for the content message: e.g. H&W coaches, other coaches, philanthropic managers*

Message type: *(Course description/announcement, company news, industry news/trends, partner news/announcements, curriculum discussion)*

Key Message: *Single sentence describing the primary news/announcement.*

Support elements: *The elements explaining and defining courses, company news, etc. e.g. – instructor bios, course details, backgrounds, etc. to help readers understand the content announcement and how it can help them.*

The goal is to get a post of roughly 100-130 words.

Salesboxer

Figure A3

Sample Questions and Solicitation E-mail for a Social Media Panel

A panel on social media is a great way to get businesses talking with one another about the best practices to use. Social media for business is relatively new for all of us, so we should dive in together. We've put below sample questions and a sample solicitation e-mail to get a social media panel put together in your area.

Sample Questions for a Social Media Panel

1. Why do you use social media for your business?
2. What's your favorite social media platform and why?
3. What types of posts engage people the most?
4. Do you have a daily/weekly/monthly plan for social media and posting times?
5. When did your platforms really start taking off with followers?
6. Do you get leads and legitimate business from your social media posts?
7. What do you think will be the future of social media for businesses?
8. How do you motivate and continue to engage your followers on social media?
9. Is there anything else you would like to add?

Sample Solicitation E-mail for a Social Media Panel for Chambers of Commerce

Dear Members,

We have a great year ahead of us for our scheduled programming. One of these events will include a panel from our members around setting up and maintaining social media for your business. We will feature a book called *Make Your Business Social* and would like to have at least four of our members serve on the panel. If you have successfully set up social media for your business and want to help the Chamber's members with your answers and knowledge, we would be thrilled to feature you.

Please let me know if you would like to be on our panel.

About the Authors

Lindsay Chambers is a marketing content specialist. In her role as project manager with Salesboxer, Chambers oversees the creation, placement, and management of Facebook ads for multiple clients. She also creates and sends e-mail marketing campaigns and manages client relationships to ensure they are happy and that Salesboxer is fulfilling their needs.

Jennifer Morehead is an entrepreneur, sales and marketing expert, independent board member, private investor, and fundraiser. She successfully founded Salesboxer, which provides marketing solutions for local businesses throughout the country. Morehead is passionate about providing local businesses with effective tools to help them find new customers and maintain engagement with their current customers.

Heather Sallee is the CEO of Salesboxer. Throughout her career, she has worked with companies in the initial stages of their marketing journey and also with well-established companies that needed to overcome negative reviews. With Salesboxer, she provides written content for blogs, e-mails, and social media posts to help create an image that is up front, positive, and informative for each client's targeted demographic.

Index

OTHER TITLES IN OUR DIGITAL AND SOCIAL MEDIA MARKETING AND ADVERTISING COLLECTION

Vicky Crittenden, Babson College, *Editor*

- *Digital Marketing Management: A Handbook for the Current (or Future) CEO* by Debra Zahay
- *Social Media Marketing: Strategies in Utilizing Consumer-Generated Content, 2e* by Emi Moriuchi
- *Tell Me About Yourself: Personal Branding and Social Media Recruiting in the Brave New Online World* by Stavros Papakonstantinidis
- *#Share: How to Mobilize Social Word of Mouth (sWOM)* by Natalie T. Wood
- *Digital Branding Fever* by Athanasios Poulis
- *The Seven Principles of Digital Business Strategy* by Niall McKeown
- *M-Powering Marketing in a Mobile World* by Syagnik Banerjee
- *R U #SoLoMo Ready?: Consumers and Brands in the Digital Era* by Stavros Papakonstantinidis
- *Fostering Brand Community Through Social Media* by William F. Humphrey, Jr.
- *This Note's For You: Popular Music + Advertising = Marketing Excellence* by David Allan
- *The Connected Consumer* by Dinesh Kumar
- *Email Marketing in a Digital World: The Basics and Beyond* by Richard C. Hanna
- *Corporate Branding in Facebook Fan Pages: Ideas for Improving Your Brand Value* by Eliane Pereira & Zamith Brito
- *Digital Marketing Management: A Handbook for the Current (or Future) CEO* by Debra Zahay
- *Presentation Skills: Educate, Inspire and Engage Your Audience* by Michael Weiss
- *Digital Privacy in the Marketplace: Perspectives on the Information Exchange* by George Milne
- *Mobile Commerce: How it Contrasts, Challenges and Enhances Electronic Commerce* by Esther Swilley

Announcing the Business Expert Press Digital Library

Concise e-books business students need for classroom and research

This book can also be purchased in an e-book collection by your library as

- a one-time purchase,
- that is owned forever,
- allows for simultaneous readers,
- has no restrictions on printing, and
- can be downloaded as PDFs from within the library community.

Our digital library collections are a great solution to beat the rising cost of textbooks. E-books can be loaded into their course management systems or onto students' e-book readers.

The **Business Expert Press** digital libraries are very affordable, with no obligation to buy in future years. For more information, please visit **www.businessexpertpress.com/librarians**. To set up a trial in the United States, please email **sales@businessexpertpress.com**.